LONDON'S DISUSED STATIONS

J. E. CONNOR

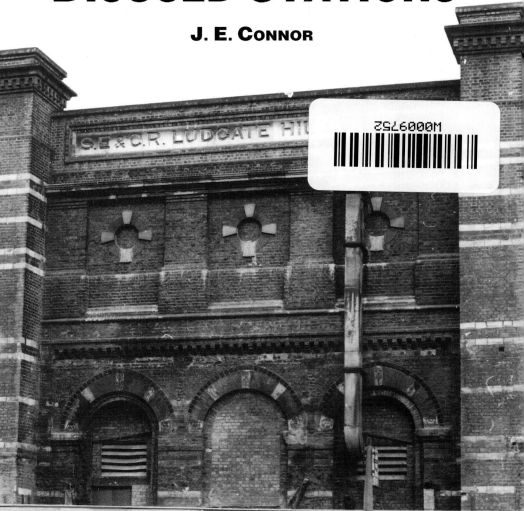

VOLUME THREE
THE LONDON CHATHAM & DOVER RAILWAY

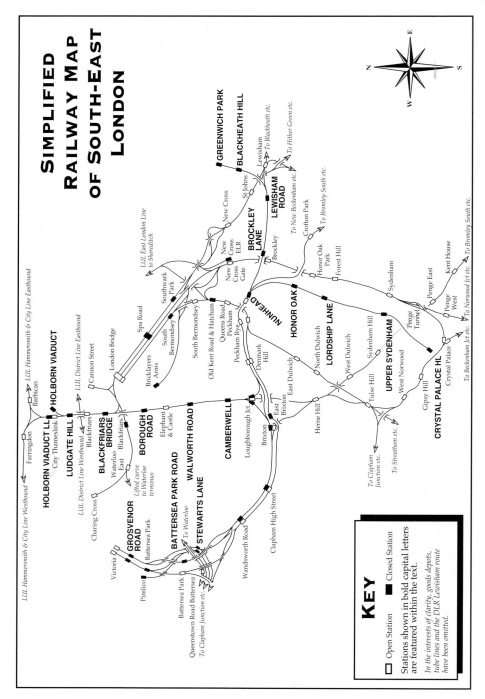

SIMPLIFIED RAILWAY MAP OF SOUTH-EAST LONDON

KEY

☐ Open Station   ■ Closed Station

Stations shown in bold capital letters are featured within the text.

In the interests of clarity, goods depots, tube lines and the DLR Lewisham route have been omitted.

INTRODUCTION

This is the third book in my series detailing the various closed passenger stations within Greater London, and follows those previously produced on the Underground system and GWR.

Before continuing, it is perhaps best to give a very brief history of the London Chatham & Dover Railway, from its formation until its eventual demise as an independent company.

Originally known as the East Kent Railway, the LCDR did not receive its more familiar title until 1859, after its extension to London had been sanctioned.

Never the most affluent of organisations, its financial situation fell to an all time low in the 1860s and led to a period in Chancery.

Its long-standing rivalry with the South Eastern Railway sometimes resulted in the construction of lines in areas already served by the SER, but ventures such as this taxed finances, which were already far from healthy.

Eventually, it became obvious that the rivalry was doing neither the LCDR or SER any good, so an agreement was reached whereby the two companies would be managed by a joint committee. Parliamentary sanction for this was received in August 1899, although the working union actually came into operation at the beginning of that year.

The companies officially retained their individual identities, but were now managed and worked as the South Eastern & Chatham Railway. This situation continued until the grouping of 1923, when the system was absorbed into the newly formed Southern Railway.

This book contains all the London stations of the LCDR which have been completely abandoned, or significantly resited, but I have intentionally omitted the original premises at Elephant & Castle which functioned from 6th October 1862 until February 1863., when replaced by the current station.

I have also omitted stations which, although still open, have lost the use of certain platforms. Of these the most notable are possibly Clapham High Street and Wandsworth Road. Although both of these are now served by the South London Line only, they originally accommodated LCDR trains as well. In fact, they were both totally owned by the London Chatham & Dover Railway, and although platforms were provided for London, Brighton & South Coast services, neither of them were actually LBSCR property. Some past writers have regarded the LCDR and LBSCR parts of these as representing separate stations, but as they came under common ownership, this was not really the case. Clapham High Street, opened as just plain 'Clapham' on 28th August 1862, but was frequently referred to as 'Clapham Road', whilst Wandsworth Road started life on 1st March the following year. The South London Line platforms at both of these were opened on 1st May 1867 and remain to this day, but those which served the LCDR closed from 3rd April 1916, when the trains which linked Victoria with Moorgate Street via Brixton and Loughborough Junction were withdrawn. The disused platforms at both stations were condemned for demolition in 1923 and removed soon after, leaving little more than gaps to indicate their former sites. At Wandsworth Road however, an intrepid enthusiast exploring the gaunt and derelict street level building in the 1970s made an interesting discovery. Stumbling over the rubble-strewn floor he found his way into the damp, dark subway which once led to the LCDR platforms. The stairways were sealed, but in the passage a white-on-blue painted sign still pointed the way to trains for either Moorgate Street or Crystal Palace. Sadly, he never had a camera with him, and when he returned a little while later, the building had gone.

Both Brixton and Loughborough Junction have lost platforms, with those at the latter being particularly noteworthy.

The first part of the station was opened as 'Loughborough Road' in October 1864. It comprised two platforms, and was located on the tracks curving round from Brixton towards the City. It was subsequently enlarged, with new platforms being constructed on both the Herne Hill and Denmark Hill lines as well. These were brought into use on 1st December 1872, when the premises assumed the name by which they are still known today. The Brixton side closed from 3rd April 1916 and were subsequently removed, whilst those serving the Denmark Hill route fell into disuse on 12th July 1925. One of these retained a building, complete with canopy until at least 1956, but although this was eventually demolished, the two derelict platforms still survive.

As with all Connor & Butler publications, I have endeavoured to include views which have not been published before, although in some cases this has not been possible. A few photographs which are of less-than perfect technical quality have had to be used, but this is due to the extreme rarity of the subject matter, and the number has, of course, been kept to the minimum.

Whilst still at planning stage, we considered placing the stations in geographical order, but before going ahead we asked the opinion of the *London Railway Record* readership. The vast majority preferred the alphabetical approach used in our two earlier volumes, so, by overwhelming request, this is the format we have used.

BATTERSEA PARK ROAD

Opened as Battersea Park (York Road) : c.5.1867. Renamed Battersea Park Road : 1.11.1877.
Closed : 3.4.1916.

A street level view of Battersea Park Road station whilst still in use. The entrance was located beneath the lamp and hanging sign under the bridge, whilst an exit can be seen on the right. There appears to have been a similar portal on the up side, which is just visible to the left of the photograph.

J. Minnis Collection

Located on the high level route between Battersea Pier Junction and Factory Junction, the station's street level access was from the north side of Battersea Park Road.

The line had been authorised in 1863 and on 1st November 1866, the London Chatham & Dover Railway informed the Board of Trade that it would be ready for opening within a month. Captain Rich carried out an inspection eleven days later, but was clearly unimpressed. In his report, written on 15th November, he stated that *"The line cannot be opened for passenger traffic without danger to the public using the same, owing to the incompleteness of the works..."* Judging from the Board of Trade file on the subject, there was indeed a great deal which remained unfinished, including alterations on the LCDR side of Victoria, which Captain Rich described as

"an incomplete terminal station at the North End of the line." Therefore, the company had no choice but to press on until the work had been finished to an acceptable standard. More inspections followed, and eventually, the route was allowed to open, with passenger traffic commencing on 1st January 1867.

The station, which later became Battersea Park Road, was still not ready at the time however, so its opening had to be deferred. On 20th April 1867, a representative of the LCDR wrote to the Board of Trade stating *"I am desired to give you notice that the York Road Station on Railway No 3 of this Company's Act 1863 is ready for inspection and to request that an officer of the Board of Trade may be appointed to inspect it within ten days of this date."* Captain Rich returned and reported his findings on 22nd April 1867: *"The sta-*

tion is still incomplete. The exit from the station is by a footpath which is raised about 4ft over the approaches and the booking office. This raised footpath is to be fenced with iron railing but the railing is not yet put up and consequently there is nothing to protect the passengers from falling over. The waste material and timber (which) is lying about should also be cleared away... The signal man at York Road Station cannot see the distant signals towards Wandsworth Road Station, which he has to work and drivers approaching York Road Station from the south cannot get a clear view of the station signals at York Road. The signal man cannot see a train approaching from the south, till it is close to the Station. The signal man's hut requires to be moved to the other end of the Station or to be considerably raised and starting signals should be supplied. I submit that the York Road Station of The London Chatham & Dover Railway cannot be opened for passenger traffic without danger to the public using the same..."

Once again the company had failed to meet the required standards and on 17th May 1867 informed the Board of Trade that it was withdrawing its intention to open. Here, the correspondence ended and there are no further inspection reports within the file. According to the noted London railway historian H.V. Borley, the station was brought into use on 1st May 1867, but in the light of the letter written sixteen days later this appears to be incorrect.

However, it can be said with certainty that the station opened as Battersea Park (York Road). It was located on viaduct and comprised two platforms. These were positioned either side of the formation and served two of the three tracks which lay between them. The down line was used by both fast and stopping trains, but the up side was segregated, with a central road for those not booked to call.

The street level entrance was located beneath the bridge and led into the booking hall. This was incorporated within the viaduct arches and from here, passengers ascended to the wooden platforms by means of covered stairways. The buildings were also largely constructed of wood and were supported at the rear by iron columns.

The station was renamed Battersea Park Road on 1st November 1877 and retained this title for the rest of its existence.

A crossover was subsequently installed a little to its south and this resulted in a replacement signal box being erected at the country end of the up platform. The new cabin was equipped with fourteen levers, of which one was spare, when inspected for the Board of Trade by Colonel Yolland on 20th February 1883, prior to it being brought into use.

As with a number of inner-suburban stations, Battersea Park Road suffered a decline due to tramway competition in the early part of the twentieth century, and it was closed in the interests of wartime economy on 3rd April 1916. It never reopened and in 1923 its demolition was sanctioned by the newly formed Southern Railway, which found a contractor willing to pay £310 for materials recovered from this and other abandoned local stations.

Nothing remains to be seen from a passing train, but the former street level accommodation on the north side of

Left : LCDR green Third Class single to Clapham issued on 9th October 1886. *Right :* LCDR Third Class single issued to the Midland Railway station at Camden Road on 27th March, but an under-inked date stamp has made the year unclear. Camden Road closed on 1st January 1916.

Battersea Park Road, adjoining the well-known Dogs' Home, still survives and continues to display some of its original features. These include typical LCDR red, white and black brickwork on the arches above the window and door apertures, together with some ornamental mouldings.

Above : A further street level view of Battersea Park Road station, with the rear of the down platform buildings to the right together with a section of the up side canopy and elevated signal cabin just visible behind.

J. Minnis Collection

Below : The street level remains of Battersea Park Road station, on the down side of the viaduct, as they appeared in the 1990s.

J.E. Connor

BLACKFRIARS BRIDGE

Opened : 1.6.1864.   Closed : 1.10.1885.

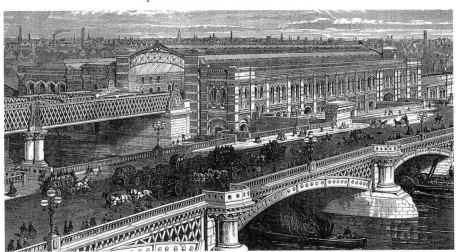

Blackfriars Bridge station, viewed from the 'City' side of the Thames soon after opening.
The Illustrated London News 26.12.1863.

The Metropolitan Extension Act of 1860 empowered the LCDR to construct lines into central London. One of these would terminate at Victoria, whilst the other was to form a junction with the Metropolitan Railway near Farringdon Street.

This latter route was carried on viaduct through the inner suburbs and eventually reached the south bank of the Thames opposite Blackfriars. Here the company erected a station named Blackfriars Bridge, which was intended for both passenger and freight traffic. The *Illustrated London News* of 26th December 1863 gave the following description : *"The work now so rapidly progressing, comprises two levels, the lower being entirely appropriated for a goods depot, the upper for both goods and passengers - the main portion of the upper or passenger level being carried on iron columns and girders. The approach to the booking-offices is by an inclined road, commencing in the new street and passing over Holland-street to the east side of the station. There are three passenger platforms, which, with their lines of rails, are included under one span of roof. There is a cab and carriage road to the arrival platforms, commencing on the south side of the new street, where it adjoins Blackfriars-road, and carried by* an inclined road on arches alongside the high level viaduct, and thence over the new street, by girders to the platforms. An entrance and exit for foot passengers is provided at the north end of the station, near the bridge, communicating by staircases with the platforms and offices. The arrangement for goods traffic, which has to be passed from the high to the low level, and vice versa, are by means of hydraulic lifts. The goods level has direct communication with the River Thames, so that goods can be landed or embarked readily. A great novelty of construction can be observed in this building by the introduction of terra-cotta, brown stoneware, and blue Staffordshire materials manufactured under Taylor's patents, the application of which is not, as has generally been the case, ornamental only, but constructive, in bands of different colours, keys and springers to arches, drip bands of brown stoneware for weathering the face of the building, copings, cornices, blocks, sills, and labels to arches all built at the time of construction with the ordinary brickwork, and being kiln-burnt and indestructible producing such an effect as the smoke of London will not easily obliterate. Terra-cotta having previously been used in this country ornamentally only, we view with pleasure this step as its use as a constructive material, successfully supplying in a* brick building the place of stone, thus making the structure uniform in its materials, and all kiln-burnt. *The variety of colour introduced is such as adds greatly to the architectural effect, and being judiciously distributed, relieves in a high degree the large masses of brickwork which are necessary to the stability of such a work. The same company has erected along their Metropolitan line minor stations of a similar description, in which the same mode of construction has been used, and with equally good effect.*" The paragraph then went on to credit the architectural work to John Taylor Junior, and the engineering to Joseph Cubitt and T.F. Turner.

The roof above the platforms had a total length of 401ft 6ins and a span of 87ft 3ins. It was supported by a succession of iron columns, placed 32ft 3ins apart, and described in *The Engineer* of 3rd January 1868 as displaying *"pleasing design"*. From the platform surface to the springing of the roof measured 22ft, whilst the height between the same level and the underside of the roof in the centre was 44ft.

The section of line linking Elephant & Castle with Blackfriars Bridge was inspected on behalf of the Board of Trade by Captain Tyler R.E., and his report dated 30th May 1864 described the formation as being double track throughout, except at Blackfriars Bridge where the tracks numbered four. The steepest gradient was 1 in 101.5, either side

of the bridge over the London Bridge - Charing Cross line, and the sharpest curve had a radius of 30ch. Captain Tyler requested a few changes to the signalling arrangements and also stated *"A bridge near the Blackfriars station is not wide enough to allow the doors of some of the carriages to swing clear of it, as they ought in my opinion to do..."* He then continued *"I have been obliged to recommend that a goods line to the east of the eastern platform at the Blackfriars station which has been prepared for use temporarily as a passenger line, should not be employed for that purpose because the platform is not sufficiently wide to be safe for the passengers."* Once his various requirements had been carried out, he saw no reason why the line should not be opened to the public, and it was brought into use almost immediately.

Blackfriars Bridge, although designed and intended as a through station, served as a temporary terminus, until the tracks across the Thames to Ludgate Hill were ready for opening.

Construction of the bridge which carried them had been delayed because the City Corporation could not agree as to what sort of design they would deem acceptable. Eventually they decided upon one of lattice girder type, which comprised five spans and would be supported by a succession of piers, arranged in sets of three. The bridge was

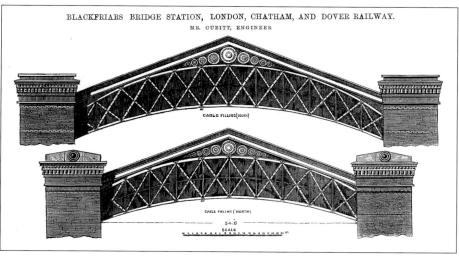

BLACKFRIARS BRIDGE STATION, LONDON, CHATHAM, AND DOVER RAILWAY.
MR. CUBITT, ENGINEER

CABLE FILLING (SOUTH)

CABLE FILLING (NORTH)

54.6
SCALE

The Engineer 10.1.1868.

Demolition of the main passenger facilities at Blackfriars Bridge nears completion as the last vestiges of the overall roof are taken down in the early part of 1886.

The SECR Society

designed by Joseph Cubitt, and stretched for a distance of 933ft. It carried four tracks and displayed the LCDR arms at its ends on large cast iron plaques. A link with the recent past was also established, insomuch as the abutments included stonework rescued from the old Westminster Bridge which had been demolished in 1861.

With the opening to Ludgate Hill in 1864 and subsequent connections onto the Metropolitan Railway, traffic increased dramatically, and the LCDR facilities serving the City soon proved inadequate. The opening of the small six-platform terminus at Holborn Viaduct in 1874 helped the situation a little, but overcrowding, particularly at Ludgate Hill remained a serious cause for concern. Eventually the company decided to erect a new station to the north of Blackfriars Bridge, with platforms for both through trains and terminators. It would also provide an interchange with the Metropolitan District Railway, which had a station named Blackfriars underneath, although the new LCDR premises were to be called St. Paul's.

As part of the planned improvements, a new river bridge had to be constructed, immediately east of the original, and provided with an extra seven tracks. It comprised five arched spans and opened to a width of 123ft at the City end to accommodate the new station platforms.

The work was authorised by the London Chatham & Dover Railway Further Powers Act of 1884, and resulted in the closure, to passengers at least, of Blackfriars Bridge station. With St. Paul's on the opposite river bank, it was deemed superfluous, but more to the point, the site of its platforms was required for necessary track alterations. It therefore closed from 1st October 1885, and demolition started soon after. It is thought that the platforms went first, followed by the overall roof, but the main building was retained and turned over exclusively to freight traffic.

Work on the alterations was completed in the following year and on 4th March 1886, the LCDR informed the Board of Trade that it was ready for inspection. The letter described the changes as extending *"from the South End of the London Chatham & Dover*

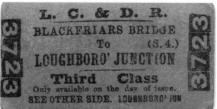

Top : Green Third Class single to Moorgate Street issued 4th August 1881. *Lower :* Green Third Class single to Loughborough Junction issued 22nd November, but year unclear.

Company's Blackfriars Station in the County of Surrey to the South Side of Upper Thames Street in the City of London and being a total length of 2 furlongs 4¾ chains."

St. Paul's station opened on 10th May 1886 and was an immediate success. Unlike Holborn Viaduct, which chiefly dealt with main line services, this was largely intended for local trains, and was frequently referred to in Board of Trade papers of the time as *"St. Paul's (City and Suburban)"*. It continues in use to this day, having been renamed Blackfriars on 1st February 1937.

The old Blackfriars Bridge station continued to serve as a goods depot until 1964, when it was closed completely. Its frontage had changed very little since its erection in the mid-1860s, whilst up above, at track level, it even retained a few of its original passenger features. Demolition came in 1968 and most of the site was subsequently used for an office development. The original bridge over the Thames, by now accommodating just one track, was closed from 27th June 1971 and demolished fourteen years later. All traffic now uses that which was erected alongside in the 1880s, but the piers of the earlier structure continue to stand, together with large cast iron plaques at the southern end which still display the arms of the London Chatham & Dover Railway. An inclined road which led from the south side of Southwark Street and curved into the goods yard also survives, complete with the pillars which once supported its entrance gates, but with the exception of a wall fragment displaying a little decorative brickwork, Blackfriars Bridge station has disappeared.

The former Blackfriars Bridge station, viewed from a passing train in 1965.

J.E. Connor

Above : An ex-GNR Class J52 0-6-0ST hauls a southbound cross-London freight past the former Blackfriars Bridge station on 19th April 1941, whilst work on reconstructing Southwark Street bridge was under way following air-raid damage.

Southern Railway

Below : A street level view of the station, taken in 1966, about two years before it was largely demolished.

J.E. Connor

BLACKHEATH HILL

Opened : 18.9.1871. Closed : 1.1.1917.

Blackheath Hill station opened as the temporary terminus of the London Chatham & Dover Railway branch between Nunhead and Greenwich Park in September 1871. It was located in cutting and comprised two platforms, accessed from the south side of Blackheath Hill, east of the junction with Lewisham Road.

The route between Nunhead and Blackheath Hill cost the LCDR a princely £450,000 to construct, having been authorised by Parliament in July 1863. The plan envisaged a line which would stretch for a distance of 2mile 18chain and terminate at Crooms Hill, on the western edge of Greenwich Park. The company started to acquire the necessary land, but progress was delayed by a severe financial crisis, which, in 1866, led to a five year term in Chancery.

Following arbitration in 1871, the LCDR was awarded enough capital to construct the branch as far as Blackheath Hill, but the section beyond here was to remain untouched and the powers to build it were allowed to lapse.

By early August of 1871, work on the initial section was sufficiently advanced for the company to inform the Board of Trade that opening was imminent and Colonel Hutchinson was appointed as inspecting officer.

His report dated 2nd September 1871 stated that the branch was 1mile 64chains long, double track throughout, and had a junction with the Crystal Palace line at Nunhead. The formation had a general width of 30ft, but was wider at stations, of which only Lewisham Road and Blackheath Hill were in an advanced state. The sharpest curve had a radius of 24chains and the steepest gradient was 1 in 78. The route included eight over-bridges, five under-bridges and a five-arch viaduct.

By and large, Colonel Hutchinson was happy with the standard of workmanship, but insisted on a number of alterations including the removal of point levers from the six-foot way at Blackheath Hill.

The station was positioned 38chains beyond Lewisham Road and was entered on a downward gradient of 1 in 82. The wooden street level building stood above the tracks at the county end and was connected to the platforms by means of a footbridge, the stairs of which were roofed over. A shelter was provided on the up side, but not on the down.

Early in the line's history, the weekday service provided a train about every forty-five minutes, with a total of twenty-six in each direction from about 8am until 11.30pm. The majority of these shuttled back and forth between Blackheath Hill and Nunhead, but a few served Victoria. Passengers using the local workings were able to reach central London by changing at the junction and joining a connecting train from Crystal Palace. A Sunday service was also provided, although there were less trains and the timetable was interrupted for around two hours in the morning in observation of church services.

Although both branch tracks may have been used initially, the LCDR issued a notice around June 1872 which read : "*As only one Train and Engine is used, the Line between Nunhead and Blackheath Hill is worked as a Single Line and all trains run on the Up Road. The Guard working the Train is the Pilotman and is supplied with a pilot badge, and no Train or Engine must be allowed to leave Nunhead or Blackheath Hill unless the pilotman gives the signal to start.*" The notice continued and under the heading "*Telegraph Signalling*" stated "*Whilst the Eastern Section Up and Down Trains run exclusively on one Line they will be signalled between Nunhead Junction and Blackheath Hill Stations only; the block needle instruments being removed and replaced by tapper bells...*" This method of working was verified by Captain Tyler, when he inspected the new Brockley Lane station, as his report to the Board of Trade written on 18th June 1872 included the following : "*...though laid with a double line of rails, (the branch) is worked at present as a single line only. The guard working the trains is supplied with a Pilot badge...*"

Perhaps not surprisingly, the route failed to attract the hoped-for custom, but the directors of the LCDR agreed that a continuation to Greenwich should put matters right. The original powers to extend beyond Blackheath Hill had of course expired, but a revised scheme to build the extension was sanctioned by

The station staff pose for a photograph on the up platform at Blackheath Hill sometime in the early twentieth century.

The Lens of Sutton Collection

Parliament in 1881.

Around this time, the frequency of trains was improved and the service commenced a little earlier than before, although the majority of workings were still of a local nature. By 1887 however, there were a few more through trains to central London, but not enough to make the line appeal to commuters.

The extension to Greenwich was slow in materialising and was not deemed ready for inspection until mid-Summer 1888. Hutchinson, by now promoted to Major General, was again appointed and his report of 13th July recorded that *"Blackheath Hill box now has eight working levers and four spare."* This appears to have been the first mention of this structure in the Board of Trade papers, as earlier reports make no references to it.

In common with the other stations on the line, Blackheath Hill was destined to be comparatively little used and the introduction of electric tramcars between Greenwich and Lewisham in April 1908 probably sealed its fate.

The branch closed in 1917, but whereas the section between Nunhead and Lewisham Road was subsequently reinstated, the stretch through Blackheath Hill to Greenwich Park remained disused and was formally abandoned by an Act of 1929. The track was lifted around the same time and the cutting was subsequently filled-in. The street level building on the south side of Blackheath Hill found a new purpose as a billiard hall, but was later rebuilt in brick, seemingly leaving little of the original still standing. Around the back, the railings which once protected the footbridge above the tracks remained however, together with a fragment of the up side stairway, but the trackbed below lay buried, virtually to the top of the erstwhile cutting. The building was used by an engineering firm, but disappeared in the late 1970s or early 1980s when the site was redeveloped for a housing scheme known as 'Robinscroft Mews'.

Green Third Class single issued 23rd January 1900.

Above : Blackheath Hill station, disused, but still basically intact, looking towards Greenwich Park around 1929.

H.A. Vallance / The Lens of Sutton Collection

Below : The street level building at Blackheath Hill was subsequently replaced by a brick edifice which seems to have occupied the same floor plan, but very little, if any, of the earlier structure. It was used as a light engineering works and the photograph shows its rear in the early 1970s. Comparison with the view above shows that the supporting girder remained and the railings along the edge of the footbridge may have been original. The cutting which previously accommodated the station platforms had been largely filled-in, but the position of the Bedford TK lorry indicates that the ground-height 'dipped' towards the former bridge.

I. Baker

BOROUGH ROAD

Opened : 1.6.1864. Closed : 1.4.1907.

Borough Road, looking towards Holborn Viaduct around 1901. Although of poor quality, this is the only photograph known to the author, which shows the station intact.

J.E. Connor Collection

Borough Road station, located between Blackfriars and Elephant & Castle, was opened with the line on 1st June 1864. The route was inspected on behalf of the Board of Trade by Captain Tyler R.E., but his report of 30th May 1864 made no references to Borough Road.

Initially built as double track, the formation between Charlotte Street, Blackfriars and Walworth Road soon warranted widening to four roads, and having carried out the necessary BoT inspection, Colonel Yolland reported on 11th July 1866 : *"A railing is required on the top of the girder-bridge adjacent to the Borough Road Station. The Signal Box should be separated from the platform by a ramp."* He went on to mention a wall at the platform end, but unfortunately his writing was unclear

and proved difficult to decipher.

The Ordnance Survey 1:1056 map of 1870 shows the station with two side platforms and a central island. The latter was longer than the others and its London end, which stopped a little short of the bridge over Friars Street (now Webber Street), accommodated the signal box. The platforms and their attendant buildings were constructed from wood, with those on either side projecting from the viaduct, supported at the rear by a succession of columns. The stairways leading from the street level booking hall surfaced behind the buildings and were possibly covered, although with lack of photographic evidence, this cannot be confirmed.

The station's fortunes were very much in decline by the early twentieth century, and *The Railway Magazine* of February 1901 contained the following satirically-tinged paragraphs by York Hopewell : *"A comparatively little-known railway station in London is that known as "Borough Road". Now, there are few folks indeed who have not heard of the "Borough" and there is a vast number of Londoners who know the famous "Borough Road" well enough. But if you ask many of them if they know the "Borough Road Railway Station," it becomes another story altogether. The suburban resident who travels up to town daily from Peckham district and onwards, is generally too much occupied with his copy of the morning paper to notice the names of stations where his train stops, let alone those where it doesn't. Ask such a man just to give you the names of the stations (in order) that he passes from Ludgate Hill to Peckham, or vice versa, and you'll be astonished at his replies. Yet he may have done the journey twice per diem, often for a dozen years!*

*So there is little wonder that, if by chance, the passenger **does** notice the name "Borough Road Station" as the train runs through it, he is simply content with that notice and troubles no more as to what sort of place this station is. For few trains indeed, stop at this London station, since it is so near the termini of Ludgate Hill and St. Paul's.*

There are two sets of lines passing through Borough Road Station - one, the main line of the London Chatham & Dover, and the other what is called the "Metropolitan Extension" line. On this latter there are a large number of trains daily, though few stop here; but on the London Chatham and Dover line the "stoppers" are even worse. An official at the station some time ago told the writer that he could recollect more than one instance where there had only been one train stop on that line during the whole twenty-four hours!...

As a proof of the "busy" state of the Borough Road Station, it may be interesting to learn that the whole staff on regular duty consists of an "inspector" (who collects tickets, shuts carriage-doors, and does lots of other things), and two lads, who help in shutting doors, carry an occasional bag now and then - when a passenger does, by any mistake, get out at this place - and shout out the name of the station to people in trains, who never under any pretence wish to disembark here. Three officials, two boys, and a man to manage a fairly large London railway station! Is there any other that can beat this record?"

By the time that York Hopewell wrote these words, the days of Borough Road station were numbered, as it succumbed to permanent closure on 1st April 1907. The wooden platforms and buildings were subsequently demolished, although exactly when is uncertain. The adjoining bridge over the main road was renewed in 1911, but the relevant papers referring to this include no mention of redundant assets in the immediate vicinity.

The former street level entrance was on the west side of Southwark Bridge Road, just north of the junction with Borough Road, and was latterly used for car repairs. Up above, a widening in the formation marks the site of the central island, and it is believed that some form of stairway access to this remained in-situ, at least until the early 1980s. At the same time, two pairs of columns which once supported the up platform were still attached to the viaduct side, but these have since been removed.

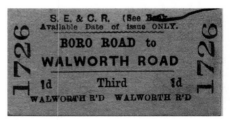

Top : Pink Third Class single to Snow Hill issued March 1898. *Lower :* Green Third Class single to Walworth Road issued 20th March 1901.

BROCKLEY LANE

Opened : 6.1872. Closed : 1.1.1917.

Brockley Lane station, looking towards Nunhead in August 1928, not long before demolition commenced. All of its signs appear to have been removed by this time, although a painted name panel survived on the up platform fence.

H.A. Vallance / The Lens of Sutton Collection

Brockley Lane station was located on the London, Chatham & Dover Railway branch from Nunhead to Greenwich Park and opened in June 1872.

The first section of this line was brought into use on 18th September 1871, but it was not until April 1872 that the LCDR was able to inform the Board of Trade that it intended to open *"A new station called "Brockley", which is quite ready for traffic."* Although provided with double track, the branch was worked as a single line at the time, so it seems that the company tried to avoid the expense of making signalling alterations. In his Board of Trade report of 18th June 1872, Captain Tyler wrote *"The Brockley station is on a gradient, as I was informed, of 1 in 80; and the view is not good in either direction. There are no signals for its protection..."* He requested that the usual station and distant signals should be provided, and these were presumably added, although the date of completion does not seem to have been recorded.

Prior to opening, the name 'Brockley' appears to have been used, but as this was the title of an existing LBSCR station nearby, a change was made to 'Brockley Lane'.

It was situated 48chains from the junction at Nunhead and had its entrance on the down side, west of what is now Brockley Road. From here, a path led into a subway, from which stairs ascended to the two platforms. These were largely wooden, apart from short sections on the bridge over the road, which were brick. The track level buildings were also mostly of timber construction and stood at the London end of the station. Waiting rooms were provided on both platforms, with an office for the Station Master on the down side and a porters room on the up.

Immediately west of the platforms, the branch crossed above the route from London Bridge which lay in cutting below and accommodated the slightly earlier LBSCR Brockley station, which dated from March 1871.

Around a decade after Brockley Lane station opened, the LCDR decided to lay a couple of sidings nearby and lease them to the Great Northern Railway for use as a coal depot. These were located on the up side of the line and their addition required the installation of a signal box. The new works were inspected on behalf of the Board of Trade by Colonel Yolland early in July 1883 and he described the box as being *"nearly a quarter of a mile from south-eastern end of Brockley Lane Station"*. He went on to record that it had twenty-four levers, of which seven were spare, then continued : *"The new signal box replaces existing Block Telegraph signal box at Brockley Lane Station and means must be provided at the Station for preventing the signalman within new signal box from taking off the down starting signal without consent of the Station Master."* He also stated that the box was *"beside up line, on space between passenger tracks and sidings"* and at the time of his visit the track-diagram and all-essential clock had still to be installed.

The depot opened a few months later, in December 1883 and was subsequently joined by Martin's Siding on the opposite side of the formation. This was brought into use in 1885 and could hold thirty-six wagons. It was leased by the LCDR to the London & North Western Railway, who sub-let it to the firm of Charrington, Warren Ltd. The Great Northern depot was entered from Mantle Road and loaded carts leaving there sometimes needed a pair of horses to haul them up the slope beneath the railway bridge.

It seems that passengers preferred the LBSCR route to and from central London, so Brockley Lane station was never well used. The coming of electric tramcars in the first decade of the twentieth century killed off what little traffic the branch enjoyed and services were suspended in the interests of wartime economy from 1st January 1917.

When the war ended, the line remained dormant and in time the former entrance at Brockley Lane was leased to the Boy Scout Movement. Up above, the wooden platforms continued to stand, but within a decade of closure these, together with their attendant buildings, had become very dilapidated. Goods trains continued to venture as far as the depot, but beyond this the tracks through the station towards Greenwich Park became overgrown.

For a while it seemed that the rest of the branch was to remain disused, but in 1927, the Southern Railway announced that it intended to rehabilitate the section to Lewisham Road and build a new spur from there to join with the Mid-Kent Line. Through freight services were introduced on 7th July 1929, after the majority of platform structures at Brockley Lane had been demolished. Peak-hour passenger trains began operating over the link on 30th September 1935, but there was no likelihood of the intermediate stations being reinstated.

Responsibility for Brockley Lane goods depot was transferred from the Eastern to the Southern Region in 1949 and it remained in use until 4th May 1970. The signal box continued to be manned for a little longer, but succumbed to its inevitable closure on 7th March 1973.

By this time, all that could be seen of the former passenger station from a passing train were the short sections of brick-built platform located on the bridge, but down below, the former entrance survived as commercial premises. When surveyed by the London Railway Record in 1997, this accommodated a shop selling bric-a-brac and was seemingly complete, although the subway between the two platforms was sealed-off some years earlier.

The old entrance continues to stand, but the platform remains have now disappeared.

LCDR green Third Class single to Crystal Palace High Level issued 1st August 1898. The journey required a change at Nunhead, but this is not indicated on the ticket.

Above : Brockley Lane looking towards Greenwich Park in August 1928. The wooden platform sections and their attendant wooden buildings were demolished whilst the line was being prepared for the reopening which took place in 1929.

H.A. Vallance / The Lens of Sutton Collection

Below : A view from a little further west, taken off the bridge over the former LBSCR, possibly in the 1950s. The non-timber sections of platform located on the road bridge had survived the general demolition, as had the erstwhile station master's office on the left, which was built of brick. Access to this appears to have latterly been by a flight of wooden steps and it may have once been used as a hut for permanent way men, although this is not known for certain.

J.L. Smith / The Lens of Sutton Collection

CAMBERWELL

Opened : 6.10.1862.   Renamed Camberwell New Road : 1.5.1863.
Reverted to original name : 1.10.1908.   Closed : 3.4.1916.

The former street level building of Camberwell station, as it appeared in the early 1980s.

J.E. Connor

One of the original stations on the LCDR 'Metropolitan Extension', Camberwell opened with the section between Herne Hill and Elephant & Castle on 6th October 1862. It was constructed on viaduct and was entered by means of a street level building on the down side. This was similar in styling to that erected at other LCDR London area stations of its time, with arched windows and doorways, topped by characteristic parti-coloured brickwork.

Adjoining the station, to the west, lay a small goods depot which opened on the same day.

The route was subsequently quadrupled, resulting in the viaduct being widened on its western side. The two extra tracks were brought into use on 1st January 1866, and the station layout was amended to suit. It now had two side platforms and a central island, although the street level building remained as before. The signal box stood towards the northern end of the island and controlled movements around the sta-

tion and goods depot. By 1895, the latter comprised a couple of sidings and a shed, and was accessed from the north side of Denmark Road, near the junction with McDowall Street.

After the widening, the passenger station, which had been renamed Camberwell New Road seven months after opening, remained little altered for the rest of its days, although its suffix was dropped in 1908. All platforms were provided with generous awnings, but that serving the up local side was shorter than the other pair.

The early years of the twentieth century saw the introduction of electric tramcars, which tempted many passengers away from local railways and therefore brought a decline in receipts. At Camberwell, the annual revenue dropped from £3,800 in 1905 to just £900 in 1912. It rallied a little to £1,000 the following year, but fell to £700 in 1914, and the trend seemed irreversible.

The inevitable closure came when the Victoria-Moorgate Street service ceased in April 1916, and the premises were largely demolished by March 1924. The contractor responsible for their removal paid the Southern Railway £200 for materials recovered from both Camberwell and Walworth Road, which was dismantled at the same time.

The street level building survived, as did part of the island platform and its twenty-five lever signal box. The goods yard closed on 18th April 1964, but the box remained in use until 15th February 1970 and continued to sport a BR Southern Region green enamel 'Camberwell' name-board well into its final days.

A substantial part of its building still stands on the east side of Camberwell Station Road and has long been used as a workshop for repairing cars. Apart from this however, the premises have largely disappeared, although a widening of the formation indicates their site at track level.

Top : Green Third Class single to Snow Hill issued 4th March 1891. *Lower :* Green Third Class single to Welsh Harp issued 28th August 1898. This Midland Railway station, located between Cricklewood and Hendon, closed from 1st July 1903.

The remains of the island platform at Camberwell, viewed from a passing steam-hauled train in the 1950s. Part of the stairwell is visible to the right.

Stations UK

CRYSTAL PALACE HIGH LEVEL

Opened as Crystal Palace : 1.8.1865.
Renamed Crystal Palace (High Level) & Upper Norwood (although 'High Level' not always used) : 1.11.1898.
Suffix '& Upper Norwood' Dropped c.1923.
Temporarily Closed : 1.1.1917-1.3.1919 and 22.5.1944-4.3.1946.
Permanently Closed : 20.9.1954.

Designed by Edward Barry and built by the firm of Messrs. Lucas for around £100,000, Crystal Palace High Level was doubtlessly London's most grandiose branch terminus.

It owed its origins to the Crystal Palace & South London Junction Railway, which promoted a new line between Peckham and the popular south London tourist attraction on Sydenham Hill. The 'Palace' itself, designed by Sir Joseph Paxton, was originally erected in Hyde Park to house the Great Exhibition of 1851, but was only intended to be temporary. However, it met with such public acclaim, that various proposals were put forward, whereby it would be retained. Eventually however, the building was purchased, dismantled and re-erected away from the centre of town. The first pillar on the new site was driven in by Mr Samuel Laing MP on 5th August 1852 and within two years the imposing glass and iron structure was ready for its royal opening by HM Queen Victoria on 10th June 1854.

A station had been provided from the outset by the West End of London & Crystal Palace Railway, but the CP&SLJR venture would offer an alternative route.

It was always intended that the company would work in conjunction with the London Chatham & Dover Railway, although it was an independent concern with its own chairman and engineer. In June 1862, the two companies formalised the following agreement : *"That the CP & SLJR complete the line with stations, telegraphs etc and maintain it for twelve months to the satisfaction of the LCDR. The LCDR to work the line from the date of completion, paying rates and all other charges except those of direction and office and to maintain the way and works after 12 months. The receipts from traffic booked from any station on the Metropolitan Extension lines of the LCDR to stations on the Crystal Palace line and vice versa and the receipts from traffic earned locally upon the Crystal Palace line will form the gross receipts from which the working expenses of the*

LCDR will be deducted to the extent of not less than 50% and not more than 60%. The surplus receipts will be paid to the Crystal Palace line until they reach $4^1/2$% on the capital not to exceed £900,000 after which any excess will be divided in equal proportions between the companies."

Messrs Peto & Betts were awarded the contract for the construction of the line and by November 1862, the CP&SLJR solicitors were authorised to acquire the necessary land.

The branch was built under the supervision of the railway's engineer, Mr F.F. Turner and involved two tunnels near its country end. That closest to the terminus stretched for a length of 439yds and was named after Paxton, as it passed near 'Rock Hill', a residence inhabited by the architect, who had personally supervised the reconstruction of his masterpiece nearby.

In August 1863, Turner informed the CP&SLJR directors that work was progressing well and anticipated that the line should be ready for opening in July 1865. Unfortunately, the task of tunnelling was subsequently delayed by winter conditions, and despite earlier confidence had only been half completed by February 1864. This in turn delayed a start being made on the Crystal Palace station, as spoil removal had to wait until the tunnels had been finished.

Once this had been achieved however, construction continued apace and in June 1865, the date originally estimated for completion, the company was confident enough to apply for the line's Board of Trade inspection.

Captain Rich made two consecutive visits and his report dated 29th June observed that the *"New line commences at a bridge over Gordon Road."* It was double track throughout and there were stations at both Lordship Lane and Crystal Palace. He described the gradients as *"generally 1 in 80 or 1 in 78 with short pieces at 1 in 300 for present and contemplated stations."* Unfortunately, the company were clearly premature in requesting the inspection, as the report stated that the sta-

A view of the northern end of the station, thought to have been taken in the closing years of the nineteenth century. Sadly the negative has suffered deterioration over the years, but it has been included because of its historical interest. Part of the Crystal Palace is visible to the left, whilst on the right, a section of the footbridge leading from Farquhar Road can be seen above a single track siding. This served a loading dock but was also used as a headshunt in connection with the goods yard. The wooden signal cabin was subsequently replaced by one constructed partly of brick.

R.S. Carpenter Railway Photographs

tions were *"both incomplete as regards the buildings, the platforms, safe access to the platforms and they require clocks.... A turntable is being built at the Palace and is nearly complete... With regard to the terminal station at the Palace (which consists of two long arched covered ways, fronted with the station building) I cannot express an opinion in its present state. The iron and glass roof over one section is nearly completed, but none of the scaffolding used in erecting it is taken down. The platform is crowded with scaffolding under the station building and several scaffold poles are erected at other parts. The station building, under which the two lines now proposed to open pass, to the platforms is unfinished, and the whole front is covered with scaffolding on which men were working. The signal arrangements provided to work the two lines is quite insufficient for the station when complete, a temporary staircase and temporary passage which form access to the station are quite unsuited and unsafe for a Crystal Palace traffic."* With so little actually completed, it must have

come as no surprise when Captain Rich refused to sanction the line's opening!

He returned a month later and reported on 20th July that *"Work has been done except Lordship Lane and the larger half of Crystal Palace Station... The Company do not intend to use Lordship Lane or the incompleted portion of the Crystal Palace Station at present."*

Permission to open the branch was duly received and trains began operating on 1st August 1865. These ran from Victoria and left the London, Brighton & South Coast Railway 18ch east of Peckham Rye at Cow Lane Junction. They then climbed towards the Palace, but until 1st September 1865, when Lordship Lane opened, there were no intermediate stations.

As is apparent from Captain Rich's report, the Crystal Palace terminus was still unfinished at its time of opening, so only half of it was in use. One of the features which awaited completion was a 40ft wide Byzantine-styled subway, which was to give First Class passengers direct access from the northern end of the station into the Palace's central transept. No expense was spared on its construction and master-craftsmen were brought over from Italy specifically for the task.

Eventually the work was completed and as the scaffolding was removed, the impressive structure could at last be fully appreciated. It was constructed in red and yellow brick and had towers positioned at each of its four corners. From the tops of these rose a succession of square turrets, with pinnacled roofs, which created extra height and added an air of distinction.

At its southern end, the frontage faced onto Farquhar Road and included a doorway which provided access. From here, passengers entered a short passageway, then descended a flight of around eleven stairs to reach the various station facilities and offices. To the right lay a refreshment room, the booking hall and ladies, whilst to the left could be found the gents and a Third Class dining room. The central steps also led onto a gallery, which in addition to acting as a footbridge above the tracks below, also served a small side entrance which stood on Crystal Palace Parade. This was linked to the gallery by means of a stairway and proved

popular with those visiting the South Transept of the 'Palace', which was located on the opposite side of the road.

Similar facilities were provided at the north end, but here they were intended for First Class passengers and were therefore more spaciously laid out. Steps again descended from Crystal Palace Parade, but there was also the subway which led beneath the main road into the Central Transept. Directly facing this was a booking office, and access to a further gallery, similar to that serving the southern entrance. Immediately after turning into this, passengers would encounter a restaurant to their right, followed by a gents, a general waiting room and a ladies. There was also a connecting footbridge to Farquhar Road, which curved round and followed the station's western boundary.

There were three wooden island platforms and each of these was linked to the galleries at either end by stairways. Above rose two spans of glazed overall roof, which stretched the full length of the premises and were supported in the centre by a wall formed of substantial brick arches. Similar walls stood along the station's western and eastern sides, although unlike that in the middle, which were built 'open', the lower parts of these

The Crystal Palace High Level locomotive turntable, separated from the station by the bridge carrying Farquhar Road..

The Lens of Sutton Collection

Above : The imposing frontage of Crystal Palace High Level station, which faced onto Farquhar Road. The doorway which served as entrance and exit can be seen in the centre.

The Lens of Sutton Collection

Below : The Crystal Palace Parade entrance as it appeared in 1954.

H.C. Casserley

were solid, whilst the upper arch sections were fitted with glazing.

At the southernmost end, the tracks continued beyond the trainshed to a locomotive turntable, set within a 44ft 10in diameter well. Although from the outset, the trains were generally worked by tank locomotives, the turntable proved useful for engines 'running-round' after arrival, as it took up less space than the pointwork which would otherwise have been necessary.

Behind the station's west-side wall lay a single track, which was provided with a loading dock and served as a headshunt for a goods and coal yard which lay to the north of the site parallel to the approach tracks. There were also some carriage sidings on this side of the line, with a couple more, used for berthing stock, opposite them.

Initially, the service comprised nineteen non-stop trains, which ran in both directions on weekdays, but for a while there was little in the way of residential traffic. Nevertheless, within a year the daily service was increased to thirty-three return journeys, but even at this early stage, public enthusiasm for the 'Palace' was beginning to wane. The situation worsened when a fire broke out in the Northern Transept during 1866 and left it completely destroyed.

Such problems seriously blighted the finances of the CP&SLJR, which was also beginning to experience troubles with the LCDR. A lack of adequate signalling at the terminus resulted in the larger company threatening to withdraw its operation of the line and this situation was subsequently exacerbated by various other disagreements.

Meanwhile, the LCDR were busy further north, by constructing the first section of branch linking the CP&SLR at Nunhead with Greenwich. This was brought into use on 18th September 1871, seventeen days after Nunhead station was opened, 54ch east of Cow Lane Junction.

The bad atmosphere between the two companies continued and was brought to a head in 1874 when the LCDR obtained authority to build a connection onto the rival route to Crystal Palace, which dated back to 1854 and was now owned by the London Brighton & South Coast Railway. This meant that the 'Palace' could be served from both Victoria and the newly opened Holborn Viaduct,

without using the CP&SLJR branch, therefore effectively leaving it without trains. The Crystal Palace & South London Junction Railway realised that it was facing an ultimatum and the Board decided to take the only viable option. They agreed to sell out to the larger organisation and their undertaking was officially absorbed into the LCDR in 1875.

By the beginning of 1877, there were twenty-four weekday trains from Victoria to Crystal Palace between 6.55am and 10.52pm, of which one ran non-stop and covered the journey in twenty-five minutes. There were also thirty trains originating from the Metropolitan Extension, with some completing the run in less than half an hour.

As time progressed, additional stations were opened on the branch, with the first at Honor Oak as early as December 1865 and the second at Upper Sydenham nineteen years later. These, together with Lordship Lane, all catered for the needs of residential traffic, but the terminus was still chiefly used by the declining number of people who wished to visit the Crystal Palace.

The station was renamed Crystal Palace (High Level) & Upper Norwood on 1st November 1898, no doubt in an attempt to

At the start of the 1920s, a pair of SECR railmotors were stored at Crystal Palace High Level, having been declared surplus to requirements elsewhere on the system. This view shows one of them, with a section of the palace visible above the retaining wall to the left.
The Lens of Sutton Collection

The west side of the station, looking towards Nunhead around 1954, with the dividing wall which separated it from the eastern platforms on the right.

The Lens of Sutton Collection

drum up more use by commuters, but it wasn't a great success.

The Crystal Palace offered an excellent venue for various special events, but as the new century dawned these were becoming less and less. The FA Cup Final was held in the grounds from 1894 until 1914 and The Festival of Empire and Imperial Exhibition of 1911 also proved very popular. At times like this, the ample station came into its own, and the line proved its worth. During the 1911 Show, which ran between March and October, trains formed of ten four-wheel coaches covered the distance between Victoria and Crystal Palace in a quarter of an hour, which was two minutes faster than the newly electrified LBSCR route linking the same points. On one day of the event, a King's Fete was held, which required the operation of forty-seven special trains, full of school children, in and out of Crystal Palace (High Level). To cope with this influx, ninety extra staff were brought in to work at the terminus and sixty-one out of the regular ninety-eight services had to be cancelled to provide the necessary pathways.

In 1914, the 'Palace' itself was taken over by the Admiralty to be used as a recruiting and training centre. By this time, the residential traffic which previously had used the stations at Honor Oak and Lordship Lane had been eroded by tramway competition, so the branch seemed an ideal candidate for wartime economies. The services over the Metropolitan Extension into Moorgate Street were reduced in January 1915 and ceased completely in April of the following year. This left just the Victoria trains, which soldiered on until the beginning of 1917, when they were suspended for the duration. For a time, steam railcars, redundant from elsewhere, were worked down the branch and placed into storage outside the station.

The branch eventually re-opened on 1st March 1919, but the service only operated to and from St Paul's and Ludgate Hill, as both the Moorgate Street and Victoria trains had been withdrawn for good.

A proposal to electrify the line was made in 1920, but nothing happened until after it became part of the Southern Railway three years later. Conductor rails were subsequently laid and electric multiple-units began operating for staff training purposes between Nunhead and Crystal Palace on 1st April 1925. The full public service over the line was introduced three months later on 12th July, with trains every twenty minutes on weekdays, and every half-hour on Sunday. These ran to and from St. Paul's, which was renamed Blackfriars in 1937 and completed the journey in twenty-five minutes, having called at all intermediate stations.

Unfortunately, electrification did not bring the up-turn in traffic receipts that the Southern Railway had hoped for. During a traffic survey held during February 1926, it was found that each train left the terminus carrying an average of just thirteen passengers and the numbers at Upper Sydenham were also very disappointing. Therefore from 19th July 1926, the service was reduced to half-hourly on Saturday afternoons after 3pm, although no other changes were deemed necessary.

On the night of 30th November 1936, a fire broke out near the Egyptian Room in the 'Palace' and within thirty minutes, the great glass building was engulfed in flames from end to end. It was the most spectacular conflagration in Britain for many years and the glow in the sky could be clearly seen for many miles around. People turned-out in crowds to witness the spectacle and numbers of these climbed onto the roofs of old LCDR six-wheeled coaches which were stored near the High Level station. Although only separated from the fire by the width of Crystal Palace Parade, the old terminus remained unscathed and when all the excitement was over, the Southern Railway laid on a special train to take many of the spectators home.

Ninety fire engines and five-hundred firemen were engaged in fighting the blaze, but they were unable to save most of the structure, which dissolved into a huge molten mass in the ferocious heat. All that remained standing were a pair of 284ft high towers and a few ruined footings. With the 'Palace' died any hope of a revival to the High Level station and it fell

into a period of terminal decline, with matters worsened by the onset of war in 1939.

From 1st January 1940, the Sunday and off-peak weekdays services were reduced to hourly, which was understandable, but more drastic cuts were to follow. Through workings to and from central London were withdrawn after 6th January 1941 and replaced by a shuttle from Nunhead, which connected with Catford Loop Line trains. This arrangement lasted until 21st May 1944, when, in the interests of economy, the branch passenger service was suspended completely.

Nearly two months later, on 13th July, a bridge at Cow Lane was hit by a V1 flying bomb and destroyed. A temporary replacement was soon installed by the Royal Engineers and traffic was able to be reinstated in just ten days. Although the line had been closed to public services, the sidings at Crystal Palace (High Level) were used for stock storage and at the time contained a number of Pullman cars, which were surplus to needs due to wartime circumstances. At the same time, 5-BEL pullman unit No 3052 which had been damaged by enemy action outside Victoria, was stored beneath the overall roof. The High Level station survived the raids largely unscathed, although the pounding of nearby anti-aircraft guns destroyed some of its glazing.

The branch shuttles linking Crystal Palace with Nunhead were restored on 4th March 1946, with rush-hour Blackfriars through trains following five months later on 11th August. A full service, running at half-hourly intervals, and supplemented with additionals during the peaks, was introduced from 27th September 1948, but the Sunday workings failed to return.

By now, the years of neglect were seriously beginning to show and the once-fine terminus took on an air of desolation. The entrance and facilities at its northern end had fallen into disuse and rain falling through the broken glass overall roof stimulated the growth of foliage around the tracks. Ferns sprung up through the rotting wooden platforms, whilst above them, nets were hung to protect passengers from

Ex-SECR C Class 0-6-0 No 31576, complete with headboards and smokebox wreath approaches the southern portal of Paxton Tunnel with *The Palace Centenarian* special train on Sunday 19th September 1954.

The Lens of Sutton Collection

falling debris. Not that there were many passengers to protect, as their numbers had been far out-weighed by the rats which now scurried around the place completed unheeded.

Plans to close the branch were announced at the beginning of 1954 and implemented in the autumn. The regular service was withdrawn after Saturday 18th September, but a final steam-hauled special was operated the following day. Named *The Palace Centenarian*, in recognition of the 'Palace' being opened a hundred years earlier, it was worked by ex-SECR C class 0-6-0s throughout. It was booked to depart from the High Level at 2.22pm, then run to Richmond for a 3.19pm arrival. After a break of nearly one and a half hours, it left at 4.48pm, then travelled by way of Kingston, Wimbledon and East Putney to Clapham Junction, where a pilot loco was coupled ahead of the train engine. It then continued through Herne Hill and Tulse Hill to the former LBSCR station at Crystal Palace Low Level, where a one minute stop was scheduled. From here the special, which was formed of pre-war stock and included a buffet car, headed past Sydenham and London Bridge to Blackfriars where it reversed. The two locos at the front were detached and replaced by a fresh pair

from the same class. From Blackfriars, the train made a direct run back to the High Level, where it was due to terminate at 7.10pm. En-route it called at Lordship Lane and Honor Oak in both directions and tickets were issued carrying the heading 'Special Last Steam Train On The Crystal Palace High Level Branch'.

Considering how little the line had been used in later years, it certainly proved popular on its final day and crowds of on-lookers watched the last train go by. It had been financed by Mr G.R. Lockie, who lived locally and organised many 'ramblers' excursions' during the 1950s. All places had been sold prior to the event, no doubt because the closure of an electrified branch line in London was very unusual. The weather was fine and ideal for photography, so fortunately the event was well recorded. The power for the third-rail had been cut off the previous night, and a number of people took advantage of this by straying onto the track, particularly at Crystal Palace High Level. Detonators were laid at various locations along the branch, and there was a great deal of whistling from the locomotives, as their drivers acknowledged waves from the lineside throng. On arrival at the branch terminus, the two locomotives made their way

A northwards view from the station in 1954 shows the goods and coal yard on the left, together with adjoining roads which were being used for stock storage. The later 69-lever signal box dominates the foreground, with the southern portal of Paxton Tunnel in the middle distance. The two tracks closest to the retaining wall on the right were carriage sidings.

The Lens of Sutton Collection

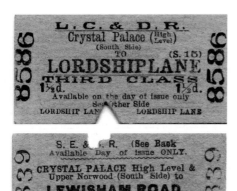

Top : Green Third Class single to Lordship Lane issued 3rd March 1892. *Lower :* Green Third Class single to Lewisham Road on the Greenwich Park branch issued 31st December 1906. Both tickets were issued from the booking office at the south end of the station.

individually to the turntable and, having turned, hauled the empty stock back to Stewarts Lane depot.

After closure, the process of decay continued, but the building remained standing, despite the removal of the branch tracks during 1956 and 1957. In the end however, it succumbed to the inevitable and demolition took place in April 1961. After this, the site lay empty, but it has since been used for housing. The brick retaining wall survives along the west side of Crystal Palace Parade, together with the subway which once connected the station with the 'Palace' itself. With octagonal stone columns supporting red and white brickwork vaulting, it provides a reminder of the grandeur that once was the old High Level terminus.

To the north of the site, beyond the erstwhile expanse of sidings, the southern portal of Paxton Tunnel remains as another obvious relic of the line. In the 1990s, a small toy-like representation of a locomotive was placed outside, but the days when trains pulled up the gradients to Crystal Palace (High Level) are now long gone.

Above : The station deteriorated badly in its final years, and the process was of course accelerated after closure. This view shows the east-side platforms, looking towards Farquhar Road bridge and the locomotive turntable, around 1956.

Below : The footbridge at the north end of the station, which had once been used by passengers travelling First Class. It is believed that the doorway at the far end led onto the footbridge link with the eastern side of Farquhar Road.

Both : Lens of Sutton Collection

GREENWICH PARK

Opened : 1.10.1888 as Greenwich.   Received final name : 1.7.1900.
Closed : 1.1.1917.

Terminus of the London Chatham & Dover Railway branch from Nunhead, it was opened seventeen years after the initial section of the line, due to the company experiencing severe financial difficulties.

The authorising Act of 1863 envisaged the line stretching for 2miles 18chains and terminating at Crooms Hill, near Greenwich Park. The original intention was to continue for an additional 2miles 52chains and terminate at the Royal Dockyard in Woolwich. At first this met with opposition from the Greenwich Observatory, but they eventually agreed to the proposal, providing the line through the park was constructed in tunnel, and all trains passing through were limited to 12mph, so as not to shake the instruments.

At the time there were three companies with their eyes focussed on Woolwich and all had viable propositions. The London Brighton & South Coast suggested a line from Peckham Rye, which would wend its way through New Cross and Deptford, whilst the South Eastern wanted to extend the existing London & Greenwich Railway. Of these, the Brighton scheme included a tunnel similar to that envisaged by the LCDR, but the South Eastern proposed taking its tracks over the park on brick viaduct. Eventually the three rival companies came to an agreement, with the LBSCR giving up all intentions to serve the area and the LCDR stopping short at Greenwich. Nevertheless, the intention to extend beyond here to Woolwich refused to die, as the Chatham's deputy chairman stated in 1863 that the company might apply to extend the route at a future date. In the following decade however, the South Eastern opened a direct line between Greenwich and Woolwich, and there ceased to be a need for the branch from Nunhead to go any further than its proposed terminus.

Unfortunately, the LCDR entered into a period of financial difficulties, and although, after many problems, the branch was constructed as far as Blackheath Hill, powers to extend beyond eventually lapsed. By the time enough money was available to contin-ue into Greenwich, local developments resulted in a change being made to the proposed terminus site. The scheme received Parliamentary sanction in 1881, but the station was now to be located in Stockwell Street, and not Crooms Hill as before.

Work was slow, but by early July 1888 the company felt it was ready for opening.

The extension continued beyond Blackheath Hill, which had acted as the temporary branch terminus since 1871, remaining level for a short distance before entering a short tunnel. It then descended at 1 in 82, passing under Lindsell Street, then plunging into a 150yd covered way, which took it beneath Blisset Street and virtually all the way to the terminus. In his inspection report of 13th July 1888, Major General Hutchinson noted that *"The Extension is double line, 43.42chains in length, entirely in cutting, the sides of which are concrete faced in brickwork."* The steepest gradient was the descent out of Blackheath Hill, whilst the sharpest curves, apart from those at the terminus itself, had a radius of 10chains. There were eight bridges over the line, all of which were recorded as having brick abutments.

The terminal station, referred to throughout the report as "Stockwell Street" consisted of a side platform and an island. These were built on a 40chain curve and were covered for much of their length by awnings. In addition to the tracks which served these, there was a central road, linked by crossovers, which allowed locomotives to be detached from incoming trains and run-round in readiness for departure. A water crane was positioned at the London end of the island and a siding for spare engines lay behind the signal box. When inspected in July 1888, this comprised thirty-nine working levers and three spare.

The main building faced onto Stockwell Street and was built of yellow brick, with segmental arches above doors and windows picked out in red and white. Adjoining the booking hall was positioned a buffet, together with ladies' room for both First and Second class passengers. The frontage was

A general view of Greenwich Park station, looking towards the buffer stops around 1928.
H.A. Vallance / The Lens of Sutton Collection

protected by a canopy, whilst set back a little, at its south-eastern end, stood a double storey house used as living accommodation by the Station Master. At the rear of the main building lay a small concourse, again covered by an awning and this provided access to both platforms.

During his inspection, Major General Hutchinson noted that the curves on the extension were not as shown on the deposited plans and described the change as being *"a very grave departure"*. This contravened the company's special Act and therefore opening had to be postponed. In defence, the LCDR stated that the revised curves were necessary to avoid private property and a fire station, but the authorities were not satisfied. On 19th July 1888, the company wrote to the Board of Trade and stated that it would approach Parliament with a view to adding a new clause to its Bill, which would cover the change in curvature. Seven days later, the Board of Trade replied and agreed to allow opening if a permanent 25mph restriction was imposed over the new line. On 13th August, the LCDR accepted the proposal and within two days, Major General Hutchinson returned to make a further inspection.

This was not the end of the company's problems however, as a letter was sent to Colonel Rich RE of the Board of Trade from a local resident, who lived in 'Bleak House', Maidenstone Hill, which read : *"I see from the newspapers that the extension from Blackheath Hill to Greenwich (LC&D Railway) is to be opened on Monday next. I do not know if your attention has been called to the condition of the walls of these premises which are not unlikely to fall upon any passing train."* The company contacted the Board of Trade on 10th August assuring them that although it was felt the wall was in no immediate danger of falling, it would nevertheless be reconstructed in the interests of safety.

With all of its problems addressed, the company were finally in a position to open its extension and services commenced on 1st October 1888.

The fact that the route to central London was very circuitous meant that journey times were more lengthy than those which were offered by the SER. Therefore the branch failed to attract many commuters, as these obviously preferred more direct, and quicker ways of getting to and from work. Even the through trains took around half an hour to reach the City and of course, a change at Nunhead made this even longer.

Top : Green Third Class single issued 16th April, but no year shown. Lower : Green Third Class single issued 28.10.1906.

Although unsuccessful as a commuting line, the branch proved useful for leisure traffic, as it provided the people of Greenwich with the most convenient means of reaching the Crystal Palace, which was then a major south London attraction. There was also a certain amount of traffic in the opposite direction, with people making day trips to Greenwich Park. However, in both these cases, the trains would only be well patronised when people had free time, whilst generally there seemed to have been little demand for them.

After the LCDR and SER joined forces as the South Eastern & Chatham Railway in 1899, the branch, which had been constructed because of rivalry between the two companies, rapidly lost any significance it might have had. As both stations at Greenwich now came under the same management, it was thought that it might be confusing to have two with the same title, and therefore the LCDR branch terminus was renamed Greenwich Park from 1st July 1900.

The traffic declined even further as a result of tramway competition, and in 1913 push-pull workings were introduced to improve economies. The line still had a reasonable service at the outbreak of the Great War, with weekday trains running about every twenty minutes in the peaks, and between thirty and forty-five minutes at slacker times. These operated between Greenwich Park and Nunhead only, and completed the journey in around nine minutes. Trains continued to operate on Sundays, but these remained less frequent, and if a prospective passenger just missed one, he or she had to wait approximately an hour and twenty minutes for the next.

The inevitable closure came at the beginning of 1917, when all traffic into the terminus ceased. After the war there was talk of electrifying the route and reopening it throughout, but this came to nothing and the tracks continued to slumber. Freight still worked into the yard at Brockley Lane, whilst surplus carriages were stored on the lines towards Lewisham Road, but beyond here the branch lay completely disused. In his book *London's Lost Railways*, Charles Klapper recounted a curious tale of some empty coaches, which having been insecurely braked at Nunhead, ran away down the branch and eventually came to a stand in the covered way between Blackheath Hill and Greenwich Park. It seems that it was some time before these were recovered, as a fortnight had passed before staff realised they were missing!

Track lifting was completed in the late 1920s, when partial demolition took place at Greenwich Park. Nevertheless, the main building remained standing until about 1968, together with a section of the erstwhile concourse. For a while it served as a billiard hall, but it was latterly used by a timber merchant, who obligingly let visitors around the back to see the various remains, although the cramped conditions made photography difficult. Three cast-iron canopy supports survived, two of which were complete with their decorative brackets, but the platforms themselves had been buried beneath a mass of in-fill. Rather surprisingly, one of the doors still displayed a poster which dated from 1916 and referred to 'The Defence of the Realm'. The majority of the frontage had been rendered and painted, but a section at its south-eastern end, together with the former Station Master's house, continued to display the colour of its original bricks.

After demolition, the site was redeveloped, and much of it now accommodates the Hotel Ibis.

Above : The platforms at Greenwich Park, looking towards Blackheath Hill about eleven years after closure. Part of the curving alignment, criticised by Major General Hutchinson whilst making his Board of Trade inspection, can be seen approaching the signal box in the distance.

H.A. Vallance / The Lens of Sutton Collection

Below : The main building at Greenwich Park, which faced onto Stockwell Street, is shown after its canopy had been removed. The view is undated, but is thought to have been taken in the late 1940s.

The Lens of Sutton Collection

GROSVENOR ROAD

Opened as 'ticket platform' : 1.1.1867. Upgraded to full station status : 1.11.1867. Closed : 1.10.1911.

A main line train from Victoria approaches Grosvenor Road station headed by a D Class 4-4-0, resplendent in her SECR livery of lined green. To the right is Grosvenor Road signal box, whilst on the left can be seen the roof of a covered stairway which provided platform access.

J.E. Connor Collection

When the first part of the station was constructed, up trains would call, so that staff could collect passengers' tickets before they arrived at Victoria. Towards the end of the year however, the premises were enlarged and brought into public use.

The street level building was located on the north side of Grosvenor Road, facing the River Thames. From here, a passageway led beneath the tracks and served the various platforms. At this point, the metals of the LCDR and LBSCR adjoined each other, having crossed the river on the same bridge. Therefore, the London Brighton & South Coast Railway had its own platforms at Grosvenor Road, but as these were regarded as belonging to a separate station, they will be dealt with in the LBSCR volume.

The narrow island platforms, which are believed to have been constructed of wood, started roughly in line with the south end of the main building, then stretched south-wards onto Grosvenor Bridge. Engineers' drawings dated 1880 and 1908 indicate that these were re-arranged at some time although full details do not seem to have been recorded.

Signal boxes were located at either end of the easternmost island. The northern cabin carried the same name as the station, but that to the south was known as Battersea Pier. When an additional crossover was installed in 1908, the existing Grosvenor Road box was demolished and replaced by a new one, recorded at the time as having fourteen levers of which one was spare.

Being so close to Victoria, the station became an early victim to road competition, with the LBSCR station closing in 1907 and the LCDR side following four years later. The platforms and their attendant shelters were subsequently removed. but the street level building was turned over to other purposes, and as such still survives today.

Above : The main building at Grosvenor Road, as viewed from the street in the 1970s.

I. Baker / Connor & Butler Collection

Below : The upper storey of the building, photographed from a passing train in 1991. This adjoined the northern extremity of the station and served the platforms by means of a subway.

J.E. Connor

Right : Pink Second Class single issued on 28th September 1911, just before closure.

HOLBORN VIADUCT

Opened : 2.3.1874. Closed : 29.1.1990.

During 1870, with a view to relieving over-crowding at Ludgate Hill, the London Chatham & Dover Railway decided to build a City terminus. £100,000 towards this venture was acquired by selling the LCDR telegraphs to the Post Office, but as more money was required, a subsidiary, The Holborn Viaduct Station Company, was formed to raise the balance.

Parliamentary authority was received on 13th July 1871, and the necessary land was acquired. Site clearance began in February 1872, with the removal of a large area of old buildings, which were described at the time as being *"unsightly and unsavoury"*. Newcastle Street, Brazier's Buildings, Turn Again Lane, Green Arbour Court, Bishop's Court, Elliot's Court, Angel Court and Sea Coal Lane were completely cleared, whilst Fleet Lane was retained but re-aligned. Sixty-three houses needed to be demolished and around eight-hundred and twenty-five people had to find replacement accommodation.

The station was designed by W. Mills, the company's engineer-in-chief and was located at the end of a new 264yd spur. The two approach tracks diverged from the existing route to the north of the bridge over Ludgate Hill, then climbed at 1 in 100 for 400ft before levelling out. Building work was contracted to W. Webster and was supervised both by the designer and R.L. Jones, the resident engineer.

The terminus comprised four 400ft platforms, of which the centre pair were islands. This arrangement provided a total of six faces, which were numbered from east to west. The station's overall length was about 750ft and its width 137ft. Protection from the elements was provided by a three-bay glazed roof, supported on lattice girders and iron columns, with ornamental spandrels. The columns rose to a height of 21ft and were positioned in three rows of twelve.

Adjoining the east side of Platform 1 was a short bay road, which served a locomotive coaling stage and a small engine shed. This had a roof-mounted tank, to supply the needs of two water cranes, which were positioned at the southern ends of platforms 1 and 2/3.

Beyond the buffer stops lay a small con-course, which in turn led to the rear of the main building. This boasted a 235ft facade, although 182ft of the total length was taken up by a covered forecourt. A range of open arches provided access to and from the street, whilst a curving road, leading from Bear Lane, brought cabs to a rank beside Platform 6.

At the western extremity of the main building was located a ladies toilet backed by the Second Class waiting room. Adjoining these to the east lay a passageway, followed by an office for the Station Master. Then came the spacious booking hall, which included a lift for the exchange of luggage to and from Snow Hill station, located on the through lines below. Next was the telegraph office and another ladies toilet, whilst behind these, facing the concourse was the First Class waiting room and a cloak room. Finally, at the eastern end of the building, came the station restaurant which was managed by the company of Spiers & Pond. On the west side of the cab rank stood a long, narrow building used as a parcels office, and behind this were rooms for guards, porters and lamps. Nearby was a 'weigh table' for luggage and another lift which provided access to the Snow Hill platforms underneath.

On 1st December 1873, the LCDR wrote to the Board of Trade and informed them that work on Holborn Viaduct was reaching completion. Initially, the company wanted to bring the station into use from 1st January 1874, but eleven days later, a further letter was sent, stating that it would not be ready until 18th February. Captain Tyler carried out the inspection and his report dated 26th February, gave the following description : *"There are six lines in the new Holborn Viaduct Station, besides certain lines for engines. A good signal-cabin has been provided at the entrance to the station, with the necessary levers in a working frame (by Messrs. Saxby & Farmer)..."* The Board of Trade was satisfied that all was well and the terminus opened on 2nd March 1874.

As intended, Holborn Viaduct began to take some of the pressure off Ludgate Hill, although most of its services were of a main line nature. Ordinary workings travelled to destinations such as Maidstone and Ashford, whilst Continental boat trains ran to Sheerness and

An early view of Holborn Viaduct, looking towards the buffer stops, thought to have been taken less than a decade after the station opened.

J.E. Connor Collection

Dover. A few suburban services used the new station, but the majority avoided it, as they continued to take the earlier low level route linking Ludgate Hill with the Metropolitan Railway. Therefore Ludgate Hill continued to suffer with gross overcrowding, particularly during peak hours, when its narrow island platforms would be thronged with commuters. In 1898, the City authorities approached the company with a view to enlarging Ludgate Hill, but were told it was not financially viable. This was seen as far from helpful, particularly as two decades earlier, the LCDR had *"found the money to build the great useless station called Holborn Viaduct."*

The signal box referred to by Captain Tyler was located beyond the south end of the station, and was fitted with sixty-two levers. It was constructed on a gantry and its rear straddled above the tracks leading to and from the Widened Lines.

On 17th November 1877, an hotel, designed by Lewis H. Isaacs was brought into use at Holborn Viaduct, and let to Spiers & Pond. It was erected above the station entrance and comprised five floors, with the upper storey windows taking the form of dormers. It served

its intended purpose until the First World War, when it was requisitioned by the Government and it was later used as the head office of Henley's Wireless Telegraph Works. Apart from the hotel, there were no other significant changes until the advent of electrification.

The station was not capable of accommodating the intended eight-car electric trains, so platform lengthening had to be undertaken. Unfortunately, site restrictions meant that only the island with faces 4 and 5 could be altered whereas the others had to remain as they were. The new services began using the station on 12th July 1925, when electrics began operating to and from Orpington via Herne Hill. St. Paul's station, south of Ludgate Hill, was less cramped, and it proved possible to extend all the platforms onto the river bridge. Therefore this took the brunt of the initial electric services, including those to Crystal Palace High Level and Shortlands.

Under the electrification scheme, the line between Elephant & Castle and Holborn was resignalled with four aspect colour lights. The equipment was supplied by Siemens-General Electric, and the existing box at Holborn Viaduct was fitted with a new eighty-six lever power frame. This was brought into use on 21st March 1926, and replaced a number of earlier cabins in the area.

As the electrified network spread, it became obvious that something had to be done about Holborn Viaduct, although this would prove problematical. Eventually however, it was decided to widen the bridge over Sea Coal Lane and extend Platform 1 to 520ft. The work was carried out in 1939, but the premises remained restricted. Drivers of incoming trains had to ensure that their units were brought to a stand very close to the buffer stops, otherwise an eight car train in either Nos 1 or 4 could foul the access to other platforms.

On 26th October 1940, the former station hotel was damaged in an air raid and was again hit on the night of 10th/11th May 1941. This time it was gutted by fire and the result was serious enough for services to be suspended until the start of the following month. It reopened on 1st June, but as the booking office had been destroyed, temporary issuing facilities, accessed by means of a passageway from Old Bailey, had to be installed.

Apart from the hotel block and frontage, the majority of the premises survived the war, including the buffet, which appeared little altered from earlier days, and continued to

exude period charm.

Everything was due to be swept away however, as part of a rebuilding scheme undertaken in the early 1960s. The ruined frontage was demolished and in its place rose an office block designed by Ronald Ward and Partners. At street level plate glass doors led to a new concourse area, which included a ticket office on its east side, a combined buffet and waiting room to the west and a bookstall in the centre. Up above, part of the first floor of the office block was used by station staff, being reached by means of stairs from the concourse. The new facilities were brought into use on 9th September 1963, but the frontage, typical of the 'modernist' style of its day failed to impress those with an interest in buildings. The overall roof of 1873-4 survived a little longer, but was removed in the spring of 1967 when replacement umbrella awnings were erected on platforms 1 and 4/5. The other platforms, not long enough to take eight-car trains were not electrified, but used for parcels traffic, which until June 1965 when it was transferred elsewhere, was fairly heavy.

The same could not be said of passenger numbers outside of the peaks however. Traffic was so light that from 14th June 1964, the station closed after 2pm on Saturday and did not

Holborn Viaduct, looking towards the buffer stops from Platform 4/5 prior to 1939, when only these two tracks were electrified. The small loco shed, topped by a water tank can be seen on the right.

Stations UK

Looking down the incline towards Snow Hill in the 1950s, with Holborn Viaduct signal box above the tracks, and the terminus to the right.

The Lens of Sutton Collection

reopen until Monday morning. This arrangement lasted for six years, but as so few passengers were using the Saturday morning trains, they were withdrawn altogether from 2nd May 1970.

Platform 2/3, which had never been lengthened and served un-electrified tracks, was demolished in 1973 and its site cleared. With that gone, it proved necessary to renumber the remaining platforms, so from 6th May 1973 the erstwhile 4 and 5 became 2 and 3. Next to disappear was the signal box, which closed from 10th March 1974, when its duties were transferred to a panel at Blackfriars. In the same year, the former Platform 6 was closed, therefore leaving the station with just three faces in operation. The buffet, located within the 1963 entrance building, and named 'The Fusilier' soldiered on until December 1979, when lack of patronage resulted in closure. It was subsequently converted into a W.H. Smith's bookshop, and a small refreshment kiosk placed on the concourse, although the latter was not destined to stay for long, as it ceased to function in 1981.

The service continued to deteriorate, with all evening trains being withdrawn after 7.30pm from June 1981. Seven years later on 16th May 1988, an even more drastic cut took place, which resulted in the station laying idle between 9.18am and 3.28pm.

For most of the day, Holborn Viaduct was now extremely quiet, with no trains arriving or departing, and just the odd unit berthed at one of the platforms. The concourse appeared desolate, and there was no sign of life, other than the occasional unwary passenger who would walk in off the street, see there was nothing running, then walk out again. There could be little doubt that the scene was set for total closure.

Around this time, work was under way on the low level route through Snow Hill to rehabilitate it for passenger use. Trains over this link, un-used since 1969, were restored on 16th May 1988, although, for the time being, there were no intermediate stations between Blackfriars and Farringdon. For a while there was talk of re-opening Snow Hill, but this was deemed impractical, so new premises were to be built instead. By then, Holborn Viaduct was clearly regarded as superfluous, with just one of its island platforms still in use. Closure was set from Monday 29th January 1990, with the last trains running on the previous Friday.

On the final evening, the normally empty concourse was crowded with people, who came to make their farewells. The ticket office, by now modernised with the computerised 'Aptis' system, was offering special edmondson card platform tickets, which had been printed as souvenirs. The last service train was followed out by an enthusiasts' special formed of corridor stock, and once this had departed, the old terminus returned to its normal empty self.

To build the replacement station, it proved

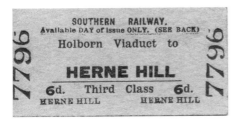

necessary to make drastic alterations to the formation, and no time was wasted in making a start. The bridge over Ludgate Hill, which proudly displayed the City crest, was now surplus to requirements, so was demolished on 13th May 1990. At around the same time, the trackbed was excavated to bring it below ground level, on a gradient, which at one point was 1 in 29.

The new station, originally named St. Paul's Thameslink, was opened in an unfinished state on 29th May 1990, initially with an entrance from Ludgate Hill only. At first the platforms were partially open to the sky, and it was possible to look up from their northern end and see the remains of the Holborn Viaduct concourse above. The former entrance incorporated within the 1963 office block was adapted to provide a further means of reaching the new station, which was subsequently renamed City Thameslink. The office block was later redeveloped, but an opening beneath the new building continues to provide access from the south side of Holborn Viaduct.

Left : *Top :* Pink Second Class single issued 1st September 1898. *Centre :* Early SR green Third Class single issued 9th March 1923. *Lower :* Platform Ticket issued 31st December 1947.

The war-damaged remains of the station frontage, prior to its rebuilding in the early 1960s.
The Lens of Sutton Collection

Above : A general view of the station soon after the office block had been erected at its northern end. Platforms 2/3 and 6 were never electrified.

British Railways, Southern Region

Below : The final afternoon at Holborn Viaduct, with only the former Platform 4/5 still in use. Almost immediately after closure, the site was cleared for redevelopment, although the 1963 office block survives and the old entrance has been adapted to serve the replacement station of City Thameslink.

J.E. Connor

HOLBORN VIADUCT (LOW LEVEL)

Opened as Snow Hill : 1.8.1874.   Received final name : 1.5.1912.   Closed : 1.6.1916.

The line linking Ludgate Hill with the Metropolitan Railway near Farringdon Street had opened at the beginning of 1866, but for a while there were no intermediate stations. This situation changed however, when work was under way on a new spur, which branched off the original route in an easterly direction and provided the LCDR with a direct link to Moorgate Street.

On 5th April 1871 the LCDR Board authorised the *"construction of a station on the company's line at the junction with the curve now being constructed by the Metropolitan Company."* Sixteen months later, the site was purchased for £12,436, and building started around October 1872.

The station was located immediately beneath the two westernmost platforms of the new Holborn Viaduct terminus which was also being erected around the same time, although a completely separate street level building was provided on the north side of the Viaduct itself. This presented a single storey above the pavement, but also included a basement, from which stairs led onto the platforms. Access was also available from the Holborn Viaduct concourse by means of stairways located immediately behind the larger station's main building.

Snow Hill had not been completed when Holborn Viaduct opened, and although technically separate from it, *The Engineer* of 3rd July 1874 described both stations as if they were a single entity. Later that month, the premises were subject to a Board of Trade inspection by Colonel Yolland and his report, dated 29th July, stated : *"Snow Hill stands on an incline of 1 in 100 immediately above the junction of the line leading to Farringdon Street Station and that leading to the (Smithfield) Market and Moorgate Street Station. No alterations have been made to the lines already authorised... The Station buildings are not yet complete, but it is thought all will be finished by the 1st August on which day the Company desire to open the new station..."* Snow Hill was indeed brought into use as planned, although Colonel Yolland had his doubts about it being built on an incline. He felt this could present a danger should there be a breakaway on a southbound working, as coaches could roll back towards Farringdon Street and block the path of a following train. A set of trailing points leading to a blind siding

was subsequently installed, and as these were fitted with self-acting switches and weighted to remain open, any such accident could be prevented.

Snow Hill's street level building, which had been constructed under contract by William Webster of St. Martin's Place, was originally fitted with a flat roof, covered in felt, which had been surfaced using tar and sand. Some time before 1886 however, an additional four floors were constructed above, and let out as commercial premises. The block became known as St Anns Chambers, with the station entrance located towards its western end, completely dwarfed by the offices above.

On entering the building, passengers encountered a short landing, then descended a flight of steps, which lay ahead of them. These led to another landing, which backed on to the rear wall. From here, stairs branched to both left and right and provided access to the gas-lit booking hall, which was situated at basement level. The same floor also accommodated toilets, a waiting room and staff facilities, and had a barrier line running across its southern side. Once past the ticket gates, those wishing to catch a train would walk down one of two stairways and thereby reach the appropriate platform. These were located partly in tunnel, but the sections open to the sky were protected by valanced awnings, supported by ornamental cast iron brackets. The northbound side was equipped with five seats at the Farringdon Street end, fitted within retaining wall recesses, whilst the same platform also accommodated a lamp bench. Toilets were provided, with facilities for both sexes on one side, but only gents on the other.

In addition to the main entrance within St Anns Chambers, there was an asphalted footpath which stretched for around 136ft and led from the east side of the building down to Snow Hill itself. Wrought iron gates, topped by a lamp, are believed to have separated this from the public thoroughfare, and it served as a supplementary means of station access. The pathway ran alongside the top of the eastern retaining wall, and led by means of a short footbridge into the booking hall. A pair of lifts were also provided, but these were only to transport luggage, and were not for passenger use.

The remains of Holborn Viaduct (Low Level) station in the early 1950s, showing platform seats in one of the retaining wall alcoves and the surviving section of awning.

R.S. Carpenter Railway Photographs

The station witnessed a great deal of traffic, both passenger and freight, as it was positioned on an important cross-London link. With all the smoke emitted from the seemingly endless stream of locomotives, it is little wonder that it got very dirty, and, according to the well-known photographer, O.J. Morris, the walls had to be whitewashed every seven days. An article by York Hopewell in the February 1901 edition of the *Railway Magazine* stated that the station was *"about as black as can be"*, and quoted a clerk from a nearby cycle shop who felt that the sign above the entrance should be amended to include *"Abandon Hope All Ye Who Enter Here!"* York Hopewell was clearly unimpressed by the facilities and continued : "There are sundry flights of stairs and several corners to negotiate after you have passed the outer portal before you find yourself on the dreary platform. The ticket-clipper has an office, adjoining the iron gate, at the bottom of the steps... Also don't be in a hurry when you have to go from Snow Hill, as the officials are very leisurely indeed, even for the South Eastern and Chatham Railway, which is saying a great deal. Altogether, Snow Hill Station is a marvel - a ninth wonder of the world - at this beginning of the twentieth century, and might well be dug up as it stands and placed in the British Museum, so that our posterity, one

hundred years hence, may see what sought of railway stations London can boast even in the year of grace 1901."

The article referred to the station as being *"little known"*, although towards the end of the nineteenth century it was extremely busy. In addition to the native London Chatham & Dover trains, Snow Hill was also used by services operated by the Great Northern, Midland and South Eastern Railways, although inter-company rivalry resulted in the latter being permitted to set down only. In the northbound direction, LCDR workings served destinations on the GNR and Midland, together with Moorgate Street, which they reached by way of the spur which branched off to the north of the station. This spur, known as the 'Smithfield Curve', had been completed before work on Snow Hill had started, and opened on 1st September 1871.

The various cross-London passenger workings which served Snow Hill suffered badly from tramway competition, and were all withdrawn by 1908. Four years later the station was renamed Holborn Viaduct (Low Level), but by then its fortunes were in decline. A census held at the station over a twelve-hour period in 1911 showed that only 2,068 passengers had alighted there, as opposed to 2,808 twenty years earlier, although the latter figure was achieved within sixteen hours, so the comparison was not strictly accurate. It was nevertheless indicative of the fall-off in patronage, as since 1908, the only surviving service was that operated by the SECR to and from Moorgate Street. On 3rd April 1916, at the height of the First World War, this was cut back to terminate at Holborn Viaduct (Low Level), then two months later, the station closed completely.

Freight services continued to trundle through however, and on odd occasions an up passenger train would end up there, having been diverted from the high level terminus. Such an occurrence happened on 29th June 1925 and was described by the Evening News : *"We passed through the gloomy underground passages past the old signs that had once directed travellers and mounted a staircase which leads into Holborn Viaduct station, and is now used, I believe, by staff. A porter was standing near the top, and as we emerged he scratched his head in amazement..."* The reason for the diversion may have been a mistake on behalf of the signalman, or it could have been because of engineering works associated with the electrification scheme. Electric trains began serving Holborn Viaduct on 12th July 1925, and conductor rails were laid along a stretch of the low level route in order to reach a sub-station.

During the same year, the addition of new toilet facilities below the high level concourse resulted in alterations to various passages and stairways, including those which led to the erstwhile station. Access was maintained by means of a door near the gents however, and this is believed to have been used by staff, including signalmen walking to and from the box which was located at the Farringdon end of the northbound platform.

By 1926 the street level entrance on the ground floor of St. Anns Chambers had found a new use as a tobacconist's shop, whilst the former booking hall in the basement served as a warehouse. Further changes came in the mid-1930s, when Stubbing & Co opened a cafe on part of the footpath leading from Snow Hill, and a part of the southbound platform was removed to accommodate catch points.

The railway historian R.A.P. Cogger recalled visiting the old station on occasion during this period, and watching the various goods trains passing through. He would descend the steps from the concourse, push open the door which was invariably unlocked, then continue onto the northbound platform, where he would make his presence known to the signalman. Thick layers of soot clung to the walls and everything was very dirty, but the premises had apparently changed little since closure. Freights ascending the gradient from Farringdon would storm through with their locomotives belching smoke which hung around the short open-air section like a perpetual fog. Behind the long assortment of wagons would come the banking engine, puffing just as furiously to push the ensemble towards Ludgate Hill, although sometimes their efforts were less earnest than they seemed. Some of the banker drivers would buffer-up to the train's brakevan at Farringdon, then move off with it towards Snow Hill. Once inside the tunnel however, they would pull back slightly, so that the loco buffers were an inch or so away from those on the van. As they started the climb they would open the regulator wide and make lots of noise, but it would be the driver of the leading engine which did all the work. This was clearly intended as a practical joke, but it also demonstrated their prowess at driving.

By the 1950s, the old station presented a sorry appearance, although it still retained some interesting features. St Anns Chambers had been destroyed during the Blitz, and with it went the former entrance. The basement which originally accommodated the booking hall survived however and remained above the tracks. From here, dusty stairways descended to the platforms, which had lost their coping and displayed makeshift wooden fencing along their edges. Sections of broken canopy still clung to their supports for a while and at least one wooden Holborn Viaduct Low Level nameboard lay discarded against a retaining wall. This surprising survival was recorded in 1948, but is thought to have gone soon after. The canopy, or what was left of it, probably went about the same time, although some of its supports lasted a bit longer.

The remnants of the street level building were also swept away, leaving a virtually unimpaired view of the station area from the Holborn Viaduct road bridge. For a while, it was possible to look over the wall and watch the various freight trains as they toiled towards Ludgate Hill, but towards the end of the 1950s, the site was rafted over and subsequently used for a new office development.

The old station was now completely under

Looking along the northbound platform at Holborn Viaduct LL in the 1950s, with a stairway which led from the former street level building visible on the left.

N. Rayfield

ground, but the platforms still remained, as did the signal box. This continued to be manned although, surrounded by the gloom of the tunnel, it must have been a depressing place to work. Trains continued to clatter through, passing the box with its tungsten lighting glowing yellow in the darkness, and its Southern Region green enamel sign displaying the name 'Holborn Low Level'.

The days of freight services using the link were now numbered however, as like their passenger counterparts of fifty years earlier, they were fast succumbing to road competition. As the 1960s drew to a close, the route witnessed less and less activity, and the last booked working, an Eastern Region parcels train, ran on 23rd March 1969. Seven months later, on 8th November, a railway enthusiasts' special formed of 6-car Hastings line DMU No 1005, travelled from its native Southern metals through to Farringdon, but after this all traffic ceased. Official closure came on 3rd May 1971, and the track was lifted soon after.

The platforms of Holborn Viaduct Low Level slumbered in the tunnel, disturbed only by the scurrying of rats, whilst the signal box lay derelict with its windows and nameboard gone. Visiting enthusiasts could just about make out the remnants of wooden seating in one of the alcoves, but it needed a very powerful torch to do so.

There could be little doubt that the line was potentially useful, and eventually a scheme was devised to re-open it. The route would allow trains off the London Midland Region of British Rail to reach the Southern Region and vice versa, and therefore form the basis of a new service to be marketed as 'Thameslink'. At first there was talk of rehabilitating the old station, but after due consideration it was decided to build completely new premises instead.

The track was re-laid, electrified, and brought back into public use on 16th May 1988, although the formation south of Blackfriars was subsequently lowered for it to pass beneath Ludgate Hill instead of over as before. Holborn Viaduct terminus was closed, and in its place a new station initially named St. Paul's Thameslink was constructed. This lay to the south of the old Low Level site, and when completed, offered access from both Ludgate Hill and Holborn Viaduct. Before building work had finished, its platforms were open to the air, but they were soon rafted over to allow development to take place above.

Despite these changes, traces of the station known for most of its existence as Snow Hill can still be seen from a passing train.

HONOR OAK

Opened : 12.1865.   Temporarily Closed : 1.1.1917 - 1.3.1919. and 22.5.1944 - 4.3.1946.
Closed : 20.9.1954

The street level building, shortly before closure.

The Lens of Sutton Collection

The second intermediate station to be opened on the line between Nunhead and Crystal Palace, Honor Oak adjoined the eastern boundary of Camberwell Cemetery.

The wooden street level building was located east of the line and included a booking hall and waiting room. It was reached by means of a short approach from the south side of West Hill Road and was linked to a subway beneath the tracks by a covered path. From this subway, stairs ascended to the platforms, which were again constructed of wood.

Apart from the terminus at Crystal Palace, Honor Oak was the only location on the branch to be provided with goods facilities. These took the form of a small yard on the up side, south of the station. To operate the points leading to this, together with a crossover between the two passenger tracks, a thirteen lever signal box was erected a little beyond the country end of the down platform.

The sidings were extended in 1924 and a year later the down platform of the station was lengthened in concrete at its southern end prior to the introduction of electric services. At the same time, the earlier crossover was lifted and a replacement laid a little further south.

Passenger traffic had been in decline since around 1907, when people began to forsake the station in favour of new London County Council tramway services. Unfortunately electrification of the branch did not bring the hoped-for increase in traffic, as a census taken in February 1926 recorded only 654 passengers joining up trains and 560 alighting from those travelling towards Crystal Palace. Nevertheless the Southern Railway continued with improvements and a passimeter booth was authorised for Honor Oak in 1929.

The street level ticket office is thought to have closed in the 1930s, when new facilities were provided at platform

Above : A general view of the station, looking south around 1954. The concrete platform extension added in 1925 can be seen at the far end adjoining the signal box.

Below : Looking south from the up platform, with the goods yard on the right and the passenger line curving to the left.

Both : Lens of Sutton Collection

Honor Oak station, looking towards Crystal Palace whilst demolition was in progress around 1956. Most of the former down platform had gone by this time, leaving just a few broken supports beside the track and the 1925 concrete extension.

The Lens of Sutton Collection

level. By then the station boasted only a single member of staff, who sufficed as booking clerk, ticket collector and porter. As up and down services often pulled in simultaneously, the man on duty would sometimes cross to the opposite platform by opening the off-side doors and stepping from one train to the other.

Honor Oak suffered the same fate as the other stations on the Crystal Palace High Level branch and was twice closed due to wartime conditions. During the Second World War, the subway was fitted out with bunks and used as an air-raid shelter, with brick screens being erected at either end in an attempt to give more protection from blasts.

Regular services ceased after traffic on Saturday 18th September 1954, but a special farewell steam train called at Honor Oak in both directions on the following day. At around the same time, a daily goods working from Herne Hill, which delivered coal to the yards, both here and at Crystal Palace, was also withdrawn, and the branch fell into complete disuse.

The station remained standing for around two years after closure, with demolition commencing just prior to track lifting. Being built almost entirely of wood, it was soon swept away. The concrete extension to the down platform, together with the adjoining signal box out-lived the remainder, but probably not for very long. By the mid-1960s, all trace of Honor Oak station had gone, although the embankment on which it once stood still existed. This was subsequently removed and the site has since been developed for housing.

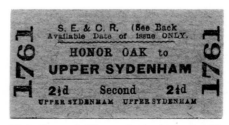

Pink Second Class single issued 10th November 1906.

LEWISHAM ROAD

Opened : 18.9.1871.   Closed : 1.1.1917.

Lewisham Road, opened in 1871, was, for a short time, the only intermediate station on the branch between Nunhead and Blackheath Hill. Its street level building was situated on the north side of Loampit Hill, close to what is now Lewisham Way, and was constructed largely of wood. This adjoined the up platform and was segregated from the thoroughfare by a small gated courtyard. A covered iron footbridge led from the side of this building and provided access to both platforms. A canopy was provided on the up side, but, according to photographic evidence and contemporary Ordnance Survey maps, it seems that the down platform was completely devoid of shelter.

In his Board of Trade inspection report of 2nd September 1871, Colonel Hutchinson noted that a drain on the up platform needed to be covered and that the shelter had not been erected. He also insisted on some fairly minor alterations to the signalling, but otherwise had no objections to its forthcoming opening. The report made no mention of there being a signal box at the station, although a notice of around June 1872, issued in connection with temporary single-line working on the branch stated : *"The signal box at Lewisham Road is closed, and the signals will not be worked until further notice."* During the same month, Brockley Lane was opened 43chains to the west and provided the route with a second intermediate station.

East of Brockley Lane, the formation descended at a continuous 1 in 100, but from Lewisham Road this eased to 1 in 263. The line was then carried on a bridge above the South Eastern Railway's main line, close to where the rival company opened St. John's station in 1873.

The branch was never well patronised, even after it was extended to Greenwich in 1888, so its closure in 1917 must have come as no surprise. Lewisham Road station was subsequently let to the Boy Scout organisation, who appear to have used both the platforms and the street level building. Although the majority of the line was completely disused, freight trains still ventured as far as the goods yard west of Brockley Lane, whilst the tracks towards Lewisham Road provided siding accommodation for stored coaching stock.

To improve freight train operations in the area, the Southern Railway announced in 1927 that it intended to rehabilitate the section of line between Nunhead and Lewisham Road and build a new

spur from there to join with the former SER Mid-Kent Line.

In connection with these alterations, Lewisham Road station was largely demolished, although the street level building was retained and continued to be used by the Scouts. At the same time, the track was re-ballasted and re-laid with new 45ft lengths of 95lb rail.

Almost immediately beyond Lewisham Road, the new 528yd loop onto the Mid-Kent Line veered to the east and parted company with the original alignment. The bridge over the South Eastern was removed, leaving just an abutment to mark its former site.

New works for the loop included a 240ft lattice girder bridge, consisting of two spans, which crossed above the main line at an acute angle. From here, the tracks were carried over Thurston Road, before descending on a gradient of 1 in 65 to a junction with the erstwhile SER just west of Lewisham station. This section paralleled the Mid-Kent Line and consisted largely of viaduct, built from brick and reinforced concrete.

At the same time another loop was added, which left the Mid-Kent route 450yds beyond Lewisham station and climbed at 1 in 70 over the River Ravensbourne to join the main line near Parks Bridge Junction.

The entire cost of the project was around £270,000, which included not only the constructional work, but also the installation of colour-light signalling.

Both loops were opened to freight traffic on 7th July 1929 and it was estimated their installation would allow the number of goods trains passing through the area to be doubled.

The loop beyond Lewisham station was electrified in 1933, but the surviving section of the old LCDR route through Lewisham Road had to wait a further two years. Passenger services over this section were introduced from 30th September 1935, with peak-hour workings linking Dartford and St. Paul's, or Blackfriars as the latter was subsequently renamed.

There were no intermediate stops between Nunhead and Lewisham however, so the remains of the two LCDR stations continued to lie dormant.

The street level building at Lewisham Road served the Boy Scouts for many years, but later

Above : Lewisham Road station viewed from the footbridge in the early years of the twentieth century, with a train for Greenwich Park waiting at the down platform.

The Lens of Sutton Collection

Below : The local troop of Boy Scouts practising semaphore at the Greenwich end of the up platform in the 1920s. It is thought that the running-in boards survived on both platforms for a number of years after closure.

J.E. Connor Collection

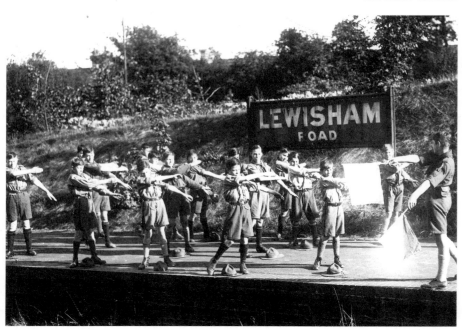

became a shop. Although it had changed hands on various occasions since, it has continued to serve this function and when visited by some of the London Railway Record editorial team in 1997 was being used for selling items of second-hand hardware. The canopy which once protected its entrance has long gone, but, externally at least, it has otherwise little changed. The lower part of the building, which was constructed from brick, faces the former up platform, but appears to be derelict. The blackened wall with its gaunt window and door openings can be viewed from a passing train, or else from the adjoining road bridge.

Above : Lewisham Road station, looking towards Nunhead in the late 1920s.
H.A. Vallance/The Lens of Sutton Collection

Left : The street level building in the 1980s.

Below : The remains of the station in 1993, with the re-routed formation curving towards Lewisham on the former SER

Both : J.E. Connor

LORDSHIP LANE

Opened : 1.9.1865.   Temporarily Closed : 1.1.1917 - 1.3.1919, and 22.5.1944 - 4.3.1946.
Closed (BR) : 20.9.1954.

Lordship Lane station, looking towards Nunhead in the 1930s.

Stations UK

The first intermediate station to be opened on the Crystal Palace High Level branch, its entrance was reached by a short approach from the south side of Lordhip Lane, just west of the junction with Sydenham Hill.

The Crystal Palace & South London Junction Railway, which was responsible for its construction intended the station to open with the line, but there were delays in completion, so on 14th July 1865, the company informed the Board of Trade that it would not be ready in time. The route was brought into use a few weeks later on 1st August, then on 22nd August, the CP&SLJR again contacted the BoT, but this time to say that the building work at Lordship Lane had been finished.

Captain Rich carried out the inspection and stated in his report that it was *"sufficiently completed to be used for passenger traffic without danger to the public"*. The report was written on 1st September 1865

and the following day, the Board of Trade officially confirmed that all was well, although by then, trains had already started to call!

The main building was designed to meet the aesthetic requirements of the Dulwich College Estate governors and stood to a height of two storeys. The ticket office was located at street level and a flight of stairs ascended to the down platform, which was constructed largely of wood. The same material was used for the up side, which was reached by means of a short subway beneath the tracks. The platforms were covered for part of their length by awnings and the up side was provided with a waiting shelter.

In 1871 it was used as the subject of a painting by the impressionist artist, Camille Pissarro, who chose a viewpoint, looking down onto the tracks from the Cox's Walk footbridge, a little south of the station.

A signal box was subsequently located a little beyond the southern end of the down side and, although this ceased to function in 1924, it remained standing for the rest of the station's existence, possibly for the use of permanent way staff. The platforms were extended in concrete towards the box in readiness for electrification, but otherwise Lordship Lane was little altered until receiving air-raid damage in the 1940s.

The branch was closed for periods during both world wars, and its final demise in 1954 was perhaps inevitable. Towards the end, Lordship Lane presented a sorry sight, with its platform awnings gone and its main building displaying the scars of war. A poster was displayed near the former entrance directing any intending passengers to the nearby ex-LBSCR station at Forest Hill, which was described as being a five-minute walk away. Demolition came in March 1957 and the site was subsequently redeveloped for housing.

For many years, Pissarro's painting was thought to represent a station at Penge, but the location was subsequently identified, and the picture is currently displayed in the Courtauld Institute Galleries which belong to the University of London.

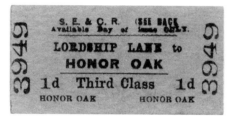

Top : LCDR green Third Class single issued on 17th October 1899. *Lower :* SECR green Third Class single issued 25th August 1911.

The exterior of Lordship Lane station, thought to have been photographed soon after closure.
The Lens of Sutton Collection

Above : Lordship Lane station as it appeared in its final days, with awnings and up side shelter removed following damage during the Second World War. The concrete platform extensions added when the line was electrified, can be seen in the foreground.

Stations UK

Below : The station in the final stages of demolition during 1957. The signal box closed when the branch was electrified, but continued to stand until the end.

The Lens of Sutton Collection

LUDGATE HILL

Opened (Temporary Station) : 21.12.1864. Resited and Permanent Station Opened : 1.6.1865.
Closed : 3.3.1929.

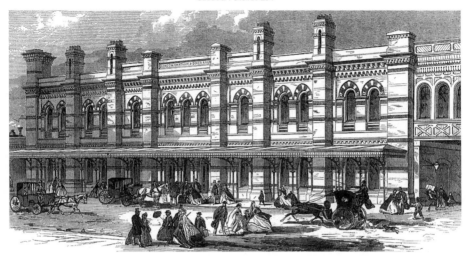

An artist's impression of the permanent station frontage, which was first published on 10th June 1865.

Illustrated London News

On 21st December 1864, the London Chatham & Dover Railway extended its services across the Thames, and brought them into the City of London. Here they were to be accommodated by an impressive new station at Ludgate Hill, but work was delayed, largely because its glass and iron overall roof had collapsed during construction. Therefore, they initially ran into a temporary terminus, which although given the name intended for its successor, was located further south and was entered from Little Earl Street.

The company obviously wanted to bring the permanent station into use as soon as possible, although it was still far from complete. Therefore, a wooden truss roof, supported by rough-cut timber columns was hastily erected to replace that which had collapsed and, seemingly without Board of Trade sanction, the premises were opened on 1st June 1865.

The facilities were far from ideal, as the site was cramped and hemmed in by existing developments. The main building together with its forecourt was located on the east side of New Bridge Street, and provided access to a pair of low island platforms on the viaduct

behind. These were constructed from wood and supported by brick walls. Unfortunately, the restrictions imposed by space resulted in them being very narrow, and at their widest, they only measured 17ft. The platform serving the up and down local lines stretched for a length of 388ft and was located on the west side of the formation. The main line island stood to the east and was 3ft shorter. Both had narrow stairways leading from the booking hall and even narrower flights of stairs serving an exit to Little Bridge Street, or Pilgrim Street as it became in 1890.

North of the station, the tracks continued towards a junction with the Metropolitan Railway near Farringdon Street, but these were not yet ready for use, so for the time being Ludgate Hill acted as a terminus.

Building the LCDR route into Ludgate Hill resulted in the demolition of numerous houses, as it cut through parts of south London which were already developed. Because many people had to find alternative accommodation, the authorising Parliamentary Act stipulated that the company had to make compensation by running trains on which special cheap tickets would be available. These tickets cost a shilling each and were valid for six days' travel. They were issued to working people of both sexes from 27th February 1865, but before they could be purchased the recipient had to give the booking clerk his or her full particulars, including name, address and place of employment. Having bought one of these, the passenger was restricted to catching one of the morning trains, which departed from Ludgate Hill and Victoria simultaneously at 4.55am, and return on one which left both termini at 6.15pm from Monday to Friday, or 2.30pm on Saturdays.

On 10th June 1865, The *Illustrated London News* reported : *"The new station of the London, Chatham and Dover Railway, and of the Metropolitan Extension Railway, near the bottom of Ludgate-hill, was opened for traffic on Thursday the 1st inst., but is yet in a very unfinished state... The architecture of the facade has no great pretensions to dignity of style, but it presents rather a lively appearance, with its turrets at each corner and its decorations of parti-coloured brickwork above the arched doorways. The interior is convenient enough for the accommodation of the large passenger traffic, which may be expected to increase considerably upon the completion of the High-Level Crystal Palace Railway and Upper Norwood station, to be opened next month, in connection with the Metropolitan Extensions of this Company's line at Camberwell. The booking-offices at the Ludgate-hill station are situated within a circular inclosure which stands in the middle of the spacious hall on the ground floor, one side being allotted to the Metropolitan Extension Railway (Brixton, Clapham, Battersea and Pimlico), while the other is devoted to the business of the main line, as well as of the Margate and Ramsgate portion, and through Continental traffic. The passengers, on alighting from the trains, may either descend the stairs to the doors opening into New Bridge-street, or, by another staircase, may emerge into a narrow lane which offers, at present, the readiest access to Ludgate-hill. When the houses yet remaining at the corner of Ludgate-hill shall be removed, a more suitable approach may be provided on that side, but it is likely that many of the passengers for the City will not alight at Ludgate-hill, but will go on by the line now under construction which is to join the London, Chatham and Dover with the Metropolitan Railway at Smithfield, thence passing on to Aldersgate and Liverpool-street."*

The company were pressing on with this extension and on 28th July 1865, the LCDR wrote to the Board of Trade and stated that it would soon be ready for use. Colonel Yolland inspected the new works on 19th August and found them anything but complete. He reported that the railings protecting the Little Bridge Street exit stairwells presented a danger as they did *"not leave 6 feet clear between the platform edges and the railings."* and went on to say *"This should be attended to as 6 feet is little enough for such a station."* He suggested that the length of the platforms should be reduced slightly, so that the stairs could have ramps either side of them instead, but he also doubted whether *"...the platforms are sufficiently wide for the traffic that may be expected."* More importantly, the junction with the Metropolitan Railway had still to be laid, so it can only be assumed that the LCDR's letter of the previous month must have been the product of over-optimism.

On 13th October, the resident engineer, Mr Thomas, wrote to the Board of Trade and stated that Colonel Yolland's requirements had all been complied with and that the company wished to commission the tracks from 1st November. However, the fact that the premises at Ludgate Hill had not been inspected as they should have been prior to opening was clearly a bone of contention. When Captain Tyler inspected the extension on 21st October he wrote *"The present notice of the Company can only be taken to include that portion of the railway which extends from the north end of the Ludgate station to West Street* (Connection with the Metropolitan Widened Lines). *The portion from the original temporary station was opened some months ago without their Lordships' sanction and is now used - although objectionable in several respects."* His report also commented on various clearance problems and, not surprisingly, Board of Trade approval was still not forthcoming.

More problems followed, but eventually these were overcome and with its connection at West Street completed, the link was finally opened. Through traffic commenced on Monday 1st January 1866 with the first northbound train departing from Ludgate Hill at 7.28am.

On the same day, a station restaurant was opened at street level, by the catering partnership of Felix Spiers and Christopher Pond. This became a very popular and fashionable eating place, despite being described by a newspaper of the time as a *"great yawning railway arch."* Spiers and Pond had previously supplied cater-

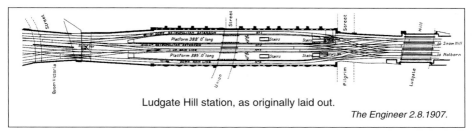

Ludgate Hill station, as originally laid out.

The Engineer 2.8.1907.

ing services to an Australian railway, but now they were turning their attention to England. They had recently introduced a refreshment room at Farringdon Street, and Ludgate Hill was their second English venture. They subsequently assumed responsibility for all the LCDR's catering requirements and did likewise with the Southern Railway until 1930.

The station was very convenient for City workers, and soon became extremely busy. Apart from London Chatham & Dover services, it eventually hosted trains off the Great Northern Railway, London & South Western Railway, Midland Railway and South Eastern Railway. However, because of the heated rivalry which existed, SER trains were not allowed to pick up passengers at Ludgate Hill, but call to set down only.

Most of the traffic serving the station was of a fairly local nature, and consisted largely of cross-London suburban workings. Those which originated from other companies reached the LCDR by means of various spurs and connecting lines which were constructed between 1865 and 1878. The link with the Metropolitan proved invaluable, as it also gave access to the Widened Lines and destinations further afield. The London Chatham & Dover provided very few of these services itself, although from 1869 its trains began to venture onto the Midland and terminate at Finchley Road, or six years later, Hendon. In 1871, a new east-facing curve onto the Metropolitan Railway was opened and this gave the LCDR direct access to Moorgate Street. As part of the agreement however, the company were obliged to run eighty trains a day over this connection, or else pay a forfeit of £30,000.

Unfortunately, money was always in short supply for the LCDR, which now found itself with a station unable to cope with its daily deluge of commuters. Being on such a cramped site, there was no room for expansion, so another solution had to be found. A new street, named Holborn Viaduct was in course of construction nearby, and the company thought that this would provide a good location for a small terminus. Raising the necessary capital proved difficult, but eventually work started and the new station was brought into use on 2nd March 1874.

Holborn Viaduct helped to take the pressure off Ludgate Hill, as far as main line services were concerned, but the suburban side was still suffering from overcrowding, particularly during peak periods. In August 1874, Snow Hill station was opened on the through lines leading to and from the Metropolitan, but even this failed to solve the problem. The conditions facing passengers waiting on the narrow wooden platforms at Ludgate Hill had become potentially dangerous, so, in 1875, the LCDR insisted that anyone using cheap workmens tickets to reach the station in the morning, had to return in the evening from Holborn Viaduct. This may have had some effect, but if so, it was scarcely noticeable. Although still hard-pressed for finance, there was little that the company could do, but build yet another station in the vicinity. This time, the site was to be south of Ludgate Hill and the new premises, named St. Paul's, were opened in 1886.

As the century drew to a close, the station received an unenviable reputation, and attracted a great deal of criticism from the railway journalist Charles Rous-Marten. In the February 1899 edition of *Railway Magazine* he wrote "*Probably no railway station since iron roads were first invented has ever come in for such an avalanche of gorgeous and whole-souled abuse as has fallen of late upon that of the London, Chatham and Dover at Ludgate Hill...*" The article, which covered five and a half pages, went on to suggest a plan for rebuilding, although the writer was clearly aware of space constraints imposed by the site. He continued "*Inside, at present, there are* four lines of rails and two narrow island platforms. *The eastern platform serves the up and down main line, which coming from Holborn Terminus, passes through Ludgate Station and then on through St. Paul's Station to the South. The western island platform has to accommodate all the rest of the traffic. Occasionally during a press of traffic a train belonging to the western platform is passed over to the eastern one, but that is the exception."* Rous-Marten's idea was to demolish both islands and erect a pair of side platforms to serve the local lines only. Although the station was largely hemmed-in by other buildings, he reasoned that it could be possible to gain extra space by demolishing the upper part of the frontage and extending one of the new platforms above the existing forecourt so that it would *"form a roof to the path"*. He also had no love for the platform covering and confidentially stated that if the scheme came into fruition *"It may be taken as granted that a new roof will be among the needful reforms effected... designed so as to dispense with the row of rough wooden columns..."* He concluded the piece by saying *"One thing more I should like to suggest. The names of our railways and stations are often much too long. Life is short and time is money, so let us avoid waste of each by abbreviating all names as much as we can. Therefore let the reconstructed station be renamed "Ludgate", and let the "Hill" disappear with other sad memories of the past."*

A year earlier, the City authorities had complained to both the LCDR and the Board of Trade about conditions at Ludgate Hill, but the company insisted that it did not have the ability to carry out improvements. Something had to be done however and early in the new century, the South Eastern & Chatham managing committee considered closure. With St. Paul's to its south and Holborn Viaduct to its north, Ludgate Hill may well have seemed superfluous, but many passengers still preferred to use it.

Eventually, the SECR decided to undertake a rebuilding, which would completely transform the place and bring it up to a more acceptable standard. *The Engineer* of 2nd August 1907 described the scheme: *"For some considerable time past the traffic arrangements at Ludgate-hill Station have not been all that could be desired, and yet we fully appreciate that under the present conditions the management was not in a position to improve them. The fault lies in the design of the building. When the station was erected, no doubt it was capable of dealing with all the traffic that was likely to be expected there, but this has now so increased as to render the present building quite unsuitable. At certain times of the day the congestion of traffic is sorely felt, and this is particularly noticeable as on such occasions when large gatherings are attracted to the Crystal Palace... The entrances and exits are small, and at times are quite incapable of dealing efficiently with the traffic. There are two platforms, one of which is 385ft. and the other 388ft. in length, and both only 17ft. wide. They are island platforms, and the whole station is covered by an old wooden roof which has done service for about forty years. The station is the property of the South-Eastern & Chatham Railway Companies, which have no fewer than seven stations in the metropolitan area. We are given to understand that quite recently it was proposed to close the station altogether, but after due consideration of the proposal it was finally decided to retain it... The station is centrally situated, and it would have caused great inconvenience to many people had the directors decided to close it... The companies own no adjacent land, and any further extensions would have involved an enormous outlay - an outlay which would not have been commensurate with the benefits*

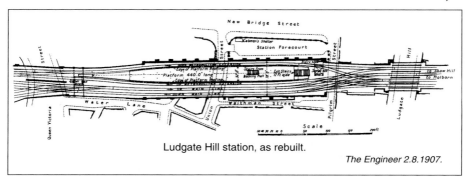

Ludgate Hill station, as rebuilt.

The Engineer 2.8.1907.

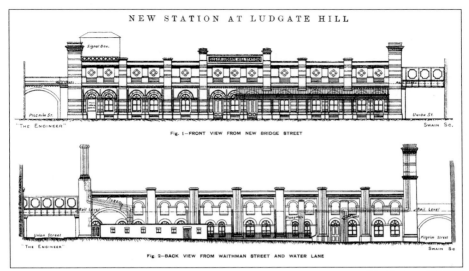

NEW STATION AT LUDGATE HILL

Fig. 1—FRONT VIEW FROM NEW BRIDGE STREET

Fig. 2—BACK VIEW FROM WAITHMAN STREET AND WATER LANE

The Engineer 2.8.1907

which the companies could have hoped to derive from it.

Briefly stated, the alterations will consist in replacing the two present platforms by one platform of the island type having ample proportions. All the main line express trains will run over the (lines laid on the former platform site) *and no longer stop at Ludgate-hill. They will pass through to St. Paul's or Holborn Viaduct. The station is not much used by main line passengers, and this new departure will not therefore cause any inconvenience. The traffic is mostly local, and is practically confined to the early morning business trains and evening traffic. The new platform will be 440ft. in length, and will have a breadth of 32ft. The platform will be covered by a roof of the umbrella type supported by central columns... it will ... .not quite extend to the full length of the platform. Another great improvement which is embodied in the new design is the size of the entrance and exit. The former is to be at least 3ft. wider than the present one.*

The work upon the alterations has already commenced, but it will of necessity be a long and tedious undertaking. The difficulties which have to be overcome are numerous, and it must not be forgotten that the work will have to be carried out without seriously affecting the handling of the traffic. Indeed, it will be impossible to close the station except on Sundays. One of the chief difficulties which has to be overcome is that of making the existing floor water-

proof. At present this is far from being the case, as anyone who has stood in the booking hall will know. It is the engineer's intention to rectify this as the work proceeds. Another obstacle almost as difficult to overcome as this will be the rearrangement of the points at both ends of the platform. This entails much work... Then, again, there is the complete removal of one platform, and the building of another, and this also without interfering with the traffic, and finally there is the removal of the present roof and construction of another..."

The old roof was supported by two rows of columns, and was bracketed to walls on either side. The modifications were designed by Percy C. Tempest and carried out by the SECR Engineering Department under the direction of W.B.S. Mills. The roof was presumably demolished first, followed by the main line island platform, as the site of this was required to accommodate a facility for works trains. On 7th July 1908 the company wrote to the Board of Trade stating a *"new temporary siding has been laid in out of the Down Main Line at Ludgate Hill station in order to allow a few trucks to be placed therein for the purpose of removing the old material necessitated by the alterations now being carried out..."* Major Pringle inspected the works twelve days later, and although generally happy with the work, requested that as the siding would be in use for the *"best part of (the) year"*, the lever for operating the points should be interlocked to three existing levers in the South signal box.

Ludgate Hill had two boxes, named appropriately, North and South. The North cabin adjoined the Holborn end of the local island platform, and was recorded in May 1886 as having thirty-four levers, of which thirty were in use. The South box was carried on a gantry above the tracks at the St. Paul's end. This needed to be fitted with a new frame when St. Paul's station was constructed in 1886 and initially comprised twenty-six working levers and two spare. At the time of Major Pringle's visit in 1908, the number had been increased to forty, or forty-one, if the temporary lever for the engineers' siding was included.

Once the main line island had been removed, the stairways serving it had to be blocked-off and filled. Before the rebuilding could commence, it proved necessary to replace the 70ft span bridges which carried the tracks over Union Street and the booking hall. Next came the diversion of chimney flues on the eastern side of the station and the waterproofing of arches. The latter proved a lengthy task, as each arch had to be stripped down to its bare brickwork, examined and re-asphalted, whilst the tracks above were supported by temporary wooden beams.

All of this was carried out with the minimum disruption to traffic however, as was the rebuilding of the surviving platform. Because of a Board of Trade stipulation, this had to be re-aligned slightly to allow more clearance on the up side. Once the old main line island had gone, the down local track could be slewed over and the platform widened. This was achieved by building brick supporting walls and providing them with a temporary surface of wooden planks. Whereas the platform had previously only measured 17ft at its widest section, it now had a maximum width of 32ft. The two stairways were also subject to reconstruction, with that leading from the booking hall being stretched to 7ft, whilst the previously narrow exit stairs to Pilgrim Street was doubled in width to twelve feet. As the side walls were no longer needed to support an overall roof, they were reduced in height to around 14ft above track level, and the finished result was described by the *Railway Magazine* as *"neatly designed"*.

Progress was hampered by the need to keep the station open whilst work was under way, and by the end of the decade much still remained to be completed. Unfortunately, since the work was first mooted, various changes occurred which were to drastically affect Ludgate Hill's fortunes. The electrification of the Metropolitan District Railway in 1905, and the extension of electric tramcars over Blackfriars Bridge four years later, resulted in many commuters deserting the station in favour of these new and more efficient forms of transportation. The heyday of cross-London suburban trains was coming to its end, and the demand for Ludgate Hill started to diminish. Between 1907 and 1909, most of these services were withdrawn, leaving just those operated by the SECR and LSWR.

In June 1910, *The Railway Magazine* published a detailed article on the rebuilding and recalled: *"For many years Ludgate Hill station has had the character of being one of the most inconvenient and unsatisfactory stations in London, and, probably, more complaints have been made concerning its arrangement, and the danger and inconvenience to passengers, than have been advanced against any other important railway station. With its low, narrow platforms, swept from end to end by the cold winds of winter, and generally gloomy and dark, the character of this station has been anything but an enviable one."* With regard to the various trackwork alterations, the article stated that *"For one Sunday in April all passenger train traffic to and from Moorgate Street was discontinued to allow of this being done, but this is the only occasion on which traffic has been entirely stopped, although at various periods certain trains have used St. Paul's station instead of Ludgate Hill..."*

At the time of the article, the temporary wooden platform was still in position, as work on its successor was described as *"one of the last things to be done"*. When complete, it would comprise tar paving supported by cross-girders and have stone coping. The report also made it clear that the new awning had yet to be fitted and the station was still *"entirely open to the sky"*.

Eventually the work was completed and the SECR wrote to the Board of Trade on 8th May 1912 informing them that the rebuilt premises were ready for inspection. Major Pringle was duly appointed and he visited Ludgate Hill a month later, on 12th June. His report written the following day stated *"The station has been completely remodelled. Formerly two island platforms*

A rare photograph of the station frontage shortly before rebuilding commenced.

J.E. Connor Collection

existed, for Metropolitan Extension and Main Line trains respectively and a single roof spanned all the station roads. *The main line platform (on the east) has been done away with, and the west platform (Metropolitan Extension) has been lengthened and widened. Formerly there was much congestion on this platform, especially in the morning and evening, owing to its narrowness. The length has now been extended from 388 to about 450 feet, and the maximum width increased from about 18 to 32 feet. Passenger accommodation in the shape of a general and ladies waiting rooms, and conveniences for both sexes, have been provided. The means of exit, formerly inadequate during rush hours, has been immensely improved by the Stairway... being increased in width from 6 to 12 feet. There is a separate staircase for approaching the platform... The platform is provided with an umbrella roof extending for a length of about 300 feet... The arrangements generally represent a great improvement upon the old conditions, and appear to be adequate."* Major Pringle required a number of signalling refinements to be carried out, and his report recorded that at the time Ludgate Hill South Box had an *"old frame"* with

forty-one levers all in use. The North Box frame had been completely renewed however and was described as having thirty-seven levers, of which five were spare.

The various signalling alterations were quickly put in hand and on 12th July 1912, the company informed the Board of Trade that they had been completed.

According to most engineers' drawings, the platform's length was 440ft, but a plan dated 1912 showed it as 449ft. This is more or less confirmed by Major Pringle's report, but when the scheme was amended is not known.

There were two buildings at track level, with that nearest St. Paul's having a length of 37ft and a width tapering from 8ft 9ins at its southern end to 12ft at its north. This accommodated a porters room, a gents toilet and a ladies room. The second building was also 12ft wide, but had a length of 27ft. This included a general waiting room, a room for the ticket collector and an inspectors office. Immediately butting onto to its north end was a bookstall, with a depth of 6ft, and counter facing in the direction of the entrance stairway. Between the bookstall and these stairs was positioned a medium sized seat, screened at the ends, whilst beyond the entrance, at the platform's northern extremity, came the exit to Pilgrim Street. The interior to the stairway was clad in white glazed bricks, illuminated by a glazed roof and windows, with that in the end wall being circular.

With its cross-London services gone, the newly rebuilt Ludgate Hill soon must have seemed like a ghost of its former self. Sandwiched between St. Paul's and Holborn Viaduct, and within easy walking distance of both, it had virtually become superfluous. The LSWR trains were withdrawn in 1916 and the station was open in rush hours only after 1919. The Wimbledon services were restored from 27th August 1923, but these only comprised four up workings in the morning and three down in the evening. After the line serving Holborn Viaduct was electrified in 1925, these were the only trains which continued using Ludgate Hill, and closure became inevitable. Also in 1925, New Bridge Street was widened and the London County Council received permission to erect a row of

shops and offices on the former station forecourt. Access to the booking hall was by a passageway between them, but the entrance was far from conspicuous. As part of the electrification scheme, both Holborn Viaduct and St. Paul's signal boxes were fitted with new power frames operating four-aspect colour lights. These were brought into use on 21st March 1926 and the two cabins serving Ludgate Hill were closed.

The Wimbledon via Haydons Road line was electrified in 1929, and as the island platform at Ludgate Hill was 80ft too short to take the new eight car trains, it was closed. The last passenger train departed at 1.50pm on Saturday 2nd March, with official abandonment taking place the following day. All of its former traffic was now being dealt with at Holborn Viaduct and St. Paul's. Neither of these underwent any major changes at the time, although the latter was renamed Blackfriars in February 1937. Another link with the past disappeared in 1938, when the Ludgate Hill restaurant, accessed since 1925 through a gap between the forecort shops, finally ceased trading, having outlived the station itself by nine years.

The north end of Ludgate Hill station, showing the top of the stairway which served the exit to Pilgrim Street. Holborn Viaduct signal box can be seen above the formation descending towards Snow Hill in the middle distance, with Holborn Viaduct terminus a little further beyond to the right.

The Lens of Sutton Collection

Above : The station still appeared to be largely intact as late as 1959 when this view was taken, and seems to have weathered its years of disuse remarkably well.

A.E. Bennett

Below : Although the frontage lay hidden for many years behind shops, the rear of the station remained clearly visible. This view dates from 1966 and includes a short section of the bridge over Pilgrim Street to the extreme right.

J.E. Connor

The frontage of Ludgate Hill station as briefly revealed in 1990, before being lost forever.

J.E. Connor

Ludgate Hill stayed largely intact for many years and even retained its platform awning. The shops erected on the erstwhile forecourt were damaged during the Blitz and subsequently demolished, but they were replaced in 1953-4 and the frontage continued to be hidden from passers-by. The rear of the station, rather plain and devoid of ornamentation, was clearly visible across a large bombsite, which, in the summer months, lay submerged beneath a sea of yellow ragwort. The catering firm of Spiers and Pond, whose Ludgate Hill Station Restaurant of 1866 had been so fashionable, still maintained a presence, as they used some of the arches at the south end of the site as warehouse accommodation. Up above, a start was made on removing the awning and by September 1960, all that remained was the skeletal ironwork. This was still there the following year, although it is thought that the platform buildings had gone by then. This rusting ironwork was subsequently taken down, leaving just the bare, empty platform, which now appeared wider than ever. The yawning, 12ft wide staircase at the Holborn end, minus its protective walls and roof lay open to the elements, with its white tiles dulled by grime and its stairs covered in rubble.

The platform was demolished in 1973, leaving a gap where it once had been, but the former frontage, still hidden behind shops, remained untouched.

The reopening of the Snow Hill tunnel to passenger traffic in 1988 and closure of Holborn Viaduct two years later, was a prelude to track

alterations, which were to change the route through Ludgate Hill forever. Early in 1990, the shops which had stood on the forecourt for over thirty-five years were demolished, and the station frontage was revealed in its entirety. Comparison with a contemporary engraving from the *Illustrated London News* , emphasised the changes undertaken during the rebuilding of 1907-12. It had been reduced in height and the upper storey arched windows replaced by blind circular insets. In doing so, a lot of the earlier ornate appearance had been lost, but eight towers, albeit truncated, continued to display the *"parti-coloured brickwork"* noted back in June 1865. In the centre, positioned between two of the towers, a large stone plaque continued to display *"SE&CR Ludgate Hill Station"* in incised sans-serif lettering, but unfortunately complete demolition followed soon after.

The formation was re-aligned, so that trains leaving Blackfriars immediately descended on a steep gradient toward Farringdon. This occupied much of the former Ludgate Hill station site and took the tracks below street level, so that they passed beneath Ludgate Hill itself in tunnel. The bridge, which was once so much part of the London scene was therefore redundant and demolished around the same time as the former station frontage. The new subterranean station, now known as City Thameslink, has an entrance which serves Ludgate Hill, but the premises, so chastised by Charles Rous-Marten back in 1899 have disappeared without trace.

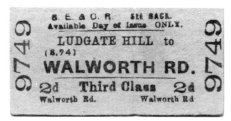 

Left : Green Third Class single to Walworth Road issued 21st April 1915. *Right :* Green Third Class single to St Anns Road issued 2nd October, but year not shown. St. Anns Road on the Tottenham & Hampstead Joint Line closed on 9th August 1942.

NUNHEAD

Opened : 1.9.1871. Resited : 3.5.1925. Sometimes referred to as Nunhead Junction.

The original station at Nunhead was entered from the east side of Gibbon Road and opened on 1st September 1871, just prior to the first section of the branch which ultimately served Greenwich Park.

The layout comprised two island platforms, which were located either side of a centre road, intended for branch terminators, but also used by through trains to central London. Sometime before 1920, the up side awning was lengthened, but no other significant changes came until the resiting. This was carried out in connection with electrification and the new station was brought into use on 3rd May 1925. The replacement consisted of a single island platform and was accessed from the opposite side of Gibbon Road. The earlier premises were demolished soon after, although traces of the entrance survived at street level.

The original Nunhead station, looking east in 1920, with the up side awning extension visible towards the far end of the platform on the right. The covered stairways which served the entrance on the east side of Gibbon Road are seen in the foreground.

The Lens of Sutton Collection

STEWARTS LANE

Opened : 1.5.1863.   Closed : 1.1.1867.

A short-lived station on the original LCDR low level route into Victoria. There appears to have been very little recorded about it, even within the files of the Board of Trade. Access was afforded by means of a footpath originating from the western end of Corunna Road onto the north end of the down platform. According to the 15in. Ordnance Survey map of 1869-70, this appears to have been provided with two buildings, with that closest to the entrance possibly accommodating the ticket office. The platforms were staggered, with the up side lying south of the down and connected to it by means of a foot-bridge. All traces have long since disappeared.

Green Third Class single issued on 22nd July, but the year has not been recorded.

UPPER SYDENHAM

Opened : 1.8.1884.
Temporarily Closed : 1.1.1917 - 1.3.1919. and 22.5.1944 - 4.3.1946.
Closed : 20.9.1954.

A general view of Upper Sydenham station, looking towards the south portal of Crescent Wood Tunnel around 1945.

The Lens of Sutton Collection

The final station to be constructed on the Crystal Palace High Level line, Upper Sydenham was positioned between Lordship Lane and the branch terminus. It stood on a gradient of 1 in 78 and had its entrance on the south side of Wells Park Road. The station house was set back slightly from the road and from here, steps descended towards a footbridge which provided access to the two platforms. According to the Board of Trade inspection report of 29th July 1884, these were *"about*

Above : The station house was reached by means of a short gated approach which led from the south side of Wells Park Road. This view is un-dated, but may have been taken around the time of closure.

Below : To the right of the house, stairs descended to the booking office and ultimately a footbridge which provided access to both platforms. The photograph is thought to date from around 1945.

Both : The Lens of Sutton Collection

145 yards long and 2ft 9ins high." The inspecting officer, Colonel Yolland, stated that *"The Station buildings are not yet complete and a clock has yet to be placed in the signal box. Otherwise I recommend to the Board of Trade to sanction the use of the Wells Road (Sydenham) Station* (sic) *for working the traffic."* He also requested that the Company should provide a pair of catch points on the down line *"a full train's length north of the south end of the down platform."* The Colonel's use of the name 'Wells Road' is interesting, but when the station opened three days later, it carried the title Upper Sydenham.

Its platforms lay within a deep cutting, in a rural setting known as Hollow Coombe. Immediately to their north was the 400yd Crescent Wood Tunnel, whilst to the south the tracks were engulfed in the 439yd Paxton Tunnel. As already mentioned under the heading of Crystal Palace High Level, this took its name from the architect Joseph Paxton.

A signal box was provided at the southern end of the down platform, and this contained levers to work the home and starting signals, but not pointwork, as there was no station crossover.

Unfortunately, traffic was always fairly light, and by 1910, thirty up trains and twenty down passed through without stopping.

The signal box was closed in the Spring of 1925 and demolished to allow platform lengthening in readiness for electrification. A sub-station was constructed nearby, which included a shaft taking power cables into Penge Tunnel directly underneath. The combined cost of this and the platform alterations came to £1,000, and technically made Upper Sydenham the most expensive station on the line to modernise.

Sadly, the new electric trains, which provided a full public service from 12th July 1925, failed to attract the hoped-for increase in revenue. During a census held on a day in February 1926, it was revealed that only 211 passengers departed from Upper Sydenham and 216 arrived.

During the Second World War, a great deal of rubble cleared from inner-London bombsites was dumped around the cutting

behind the up platform. There was no passenger service on the branch, reputedly because of manpower shortages, between May 1944 and March 1946, but during that year, heavy rain made the accumulated debris unstable. The resulting earthslip cascaded onto the station, demolishing the up side shelter and buckling the platform fence. Single line working had to be introduced, but although operations eventually returned to normal, the shelter was never replaced.

Branch services ceased after traffic on Saturday 18th September 1954, although a farewell special steam hauled train ran the following day (see Crystal Palace High Level). This called at Lordship Lane and Honor Oak, but by-passed Upper Sydenham in both directions.

For a while after closure, the station remained more or less intact. By the second half of the decade however, the surviving shelter and the footbridge had gone, leaving just the two overgrown platforms and the house at street level. The cutting was subsequently filled in and landscaped, presumably burying the platforms in the process, but the house was retained as a private residence.

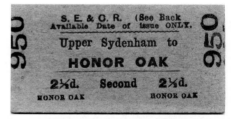

Top : Pink Second Class single to Honor Oak issued 7th January 1903. *Lower :* Green Third Class single to Crystal Palace HL issued 24th June 1916.

Looking south from the footbridge, after a land-slip demolished the up side building. White stripes on the surviving building and adjoining lamp post were added to improve visibility during the war-time black-out.

The Lens of Sutton Collection

WALWORTH ROAD

Opened as Camberwell Gate : 1.5.1863.   Received final name : 1.1865.   Closed : 3.4.1916.

A *Dawn* class 2-4-0, running tender-first, brings the City portion of the 2.45pm ex-Ramsgate train past Walworth Road station on 30th July 1900. The island platform canopy is just visible behind the signal box on the right.

The SECR Society

A street level view of Walworth Road station, with the entrance next to the Hoare & Co. public house on the right. The original print has *"Bridge 374, Down Main Side, 8.8.1912"* written on its back in pencil, and may have been taken by, or on behalf of the SECR Civil Engineers Department.

J.E. Connor Collection

The station opened at the beginning of May 1863 as Camberwell Gate. Initially it comprised two platforms, but the premises were enlarged when the route was quadrupled in 1866. Before being brought into public use, the widening had to be inspected by the Board of Trade, but unfortunately the report was largely concerned with track and signalling alterations, and made no specific mention of the station, which a year earlier had been renamed Walworth Road.

It was built on viaduct and was entered by means of a doorway on the north side of Beresford Street, or Ruskin Street as it later became. From here, stairs ascended to two side platforms and a central island. This, together with the up local side were virtually of equal lengths, but the platform serving the down main line was rather shorter. The station was supported by no fewer than three bridges, which, in order from the entrance comprised Arthur Street, Princes Street and Olney Street. The up local and island platforms ended above the south side of Sutherland Square, whilst that on the down main stopped about half way between Princes Street and Olney Street.

The signal box was located at the southern end of the central island, and, externally at least, remained little changed for its entire existence.

Although busy in its early days, the station fell victim to tram and 'bus competition, and traffic declined drastically. During 1905, Walworth Road earned a total of £6,300, but by 1912 this had plummeted to £2,300. The figure rose a little to £2,400 the following year, but by 1914 had fallen to £2,100. Despite its diminishing patronage, the station remained open until 3rd April 1916, when the semi-circular service linking Moorgate Street with Victoria was withdrawn.

The disused platforms and their associated buildings were completely demolished by March 1924.

The site of the island platform and its attendant stairwell can still be clearly seen from a passing train, but no traces remain at street level. Having said that, the facia and frieze of the public house shown in the photograph above continued to display *The Station Tavern* early in 2002, although like the premises which inspired its name, it appears to have fallen into disuse.